IMAGES
*of America*

# ELMIRA REFORMATORY

This pen and ink drawing of the Elmira Reformatory was created by architect William L. Woollett in 1871. (Courtesy of NYSL.)

**On the Cover:** Z.B. Brockway is shown watching a military drill on June 15, 1895. (Courtesy of the Chemung County Historical Society.)

IMAGES
*of America*

# ELMIRA REFORMATORY

Dr. William G. Hinkle
and Bruce Whitmarsh

ARCADIA
PUBLISHING

ISBN 978-1-4671-2037-1

Published by Arcadia Publishing
Charleston, South Carolina

Printed in the United States of America

Library of Congress Control Number: 2013934395

For all general information, please contact Arcadia Publishing:
Telephone 843-853-2070
Fax 843-853-0044
E-mail sales@arcadiapublishing.com
For customer service and orders:
Toll-Free 1-888-313-2665

Visit us on the Internet at www.arcadiapublishing.com

*This book is dedicated to my brother Patrick J. Hinkle and my sisters Jean Stark and Joan Hinkle, all of South Bend, Indiana, 2013.*

—Dr. William G. Hinkle, Chowan University

*This book is dedicated to Kathy, Olivia, and Andrew.*

—Bruce Whitmarsh, director, Chemung County Historical Society

# Contents

# ACKNOWLEDGMENTS

My coauthor and I gratefully acknowledge the following people for their contribution to this book: Beverly A. Mizen for putting the proposal together and working on the photographs and text; Ashley Salyer Thacker, Special Collections and Archives, Eastern Kentucky University; the New York State Library and Archives; Sabrina Sondhi, special collections librarian, Arthur W. Diamond Law Library, Columbia University; Jennelle Ferreira, associate editor, publications, American Correctional Association; the Chemung County Historical Society; and Polina E. Ilieva, archivist, Archives and Special Collections Library, University of California, San Francisco.

We also wish to thank our editor at Arcadia Publishing, Rémy Thurston, for his expertise, support, and patience over this long and difficult process. Rémy went above and beyond the call of duty, even locating pictures for us.

Unless otherwise noted, all images appear courtesy of the Chemung County Historical Society.

# Introduction

The most important development in correctional philosophy and practice in the first half of the 19th century was the widespread substitution, in most civilized lands, of imprisonment for corporal punishment as the usual method of punishing convicted offenders. The only subsequent achievement of comparable magnitude was the synthesis of administrative experience and creative imagination, which we have come to know as the reformatory movement. This was the second great stage in the improvement of correctional philosophy and practice in the United States.

Inspired by a philanthropic purpose and made possible by a broad-minded legislature, the Elmira Reformatory advanced beyond the ambition that had been set by its founders. From a mere modernized prison, as it needed to be in the first few years of its occupation, it had, by 1880, developed into a great compulsory educational establishment for the improvement of convicted felons.

From its foundation in 1876, the Elmira Reformatory developed in the direction of its object (to a "crime hospital" for the morally depraved) since the day of its dedication. By 1890, there was widespread public recognition and acceptance of the principles of pathological theories of crime and the treatment of criminals. These principles became the cornerstone of the reformatory's system of prison discipline. The efforts of 14 years of operation had been marked by a highly encouraging measure of success and broadened the field of action for remolding men who had been "imperfectly cast" for citizenship.

For the first decade of its existence, the reformatory was regarded as an experiment in criminology, a homogenous system of a number of radical theories developed in the minds of men who had formed a proper regard for the problem of crime. A scientific investigation of their subject convinced them that the punishment to deter philosophy encouraged rather than discouraged the formation of a criminal class. They took the view that the criminal was most often a criminal through heredity, environment, or mental and physical defects. They sought to correct those defects and, in the process, came to the rational conclusion that there were grades of criminals—first offenders, recidivists, and incorrigibles—whose treatment might profitably be tempered to their gradation. In 1890, the inmates of the reformatory were, as from the beginning, classified into three grades, which were designated as the first, second, and third.

Comparing crime to a disease, it was believed that like the patient suffering from a physical illness, prisoners should be kept under treatment until cured of their criminal propensities. The indeterminate sentence was thus established as a basic principle. The statute provided for this fell short of making the sentence strictly indeterminate by forbidding the incarceration of the offender beyond his maximum term of imprisonment. Convalescence was construed to be moral, intellectual, and physical capability to earn a living and to become a law-abiding productive member of society. The reformatory prescription consisted of a trinity of Ms—mental, moral, and manual training. These ingredients varied based on the needs of the patient as developed in diagnosis and, sometimes, by the invention of better methods and/or the intervention of new laws.

In the course of its history, the guiding philosophy at Elmira was always reform. However, the type of reform changed from the distinct emphasis on moral and intellectual reform (between 1876 and 1891) to pathological reform (from 1892 until early in the 20th century). Unfortunately, Elmira is better known for its focus on pathological reform, a school of thought that has been all but completely discredited. Consequently, the groundbreaking work done between 1876 and 1890 has been largely forgotten. Indeed, it is this early period that deserves reexamination to the extent that it was guided by theoretical assumptions that have, in fact, stood the test of time and empirical scrutiny, especially the assumption that education will reduce criminal recidivism.

Because the Elmira Reformatory was the first notable institution that embodied all the principles of the reformatory system and was devoted exclusively to youthful offenders, it was frequently asserted that the reformatory was a peculiarly American institution. However, in 1854, Sir Walter Crofton (1815–1897) based his system of convict discipline upon Captain Maconochie's plan. The Irish System, as it came to be known, was devised and inaugurated in Ireland from 1854 to 1862. Crofton brought the Irish prisons into a state far superior to those of England, introducing, besides reformatory treatment, a four-stage graduated release component. The first stage was severely penal, with nine months in solitary, no labor, and reduced rations. In the second stage, the prisoner was permitted to work with other inmates and to earn marks to progress to the third stage. In the third stage, the prisoner was sent to an open institution, where he could earn his release on a ticket of leave. In the fourth stage, the inmate was released from custody and then supervised on the outside by the police. What the American reformers did was to work out the first complete synthesis of Maconochie and Crofton's enlightened principles and to apply them in an institution that received inmates between 16 and 30 years of age.

The Elmira Reformatory's first superintendent, Zebulon Brockway, began his 50 years of prison employment as a clerk at the Wethersfield State Prison in Connecticut. The Wethersfield facility had been strongly influenced by a family of prison wardens named the Pilsburys, who had turned the prison into a giant and profitable industrial facility. Although the Pilsburys no longer worked at Wethersfield during Brockway's tenure, their influence remained. The Pilsburys always held that the profitable employment of prisoners to defray the cost of their maintenance was the main end of prison management. Although supportive of the notion of individual reform, they did not adopt the scientific reformatory methods that were championed by Brockway later on at Elmira. Their influence on Brockway, however, was significant. Brockway believed that the stringent discipline maintained by the Pilsburys was indispensable in any really effective reconstructive formation of the character of adult criminals.

By chapter 408 of the laws of 1869, a reformatory was authorized to receive male offenders between the ages of 16 and 30. The following year, the first convention of the American Prison Association met in Cincinnati. Zebulon Brockway presented a paper based on the Irish system, which dealt with the idea of an indeterminate sentence and the possibilities of a system of parole. The prison reformers meeting in Cincinnati urged New York to adopt Brockway's proposal at Elmira. When the Elmira Reformatory opened in 1876, Brockway was appointed superintendent. For Brockway, the causes of crime were to be found in class differences, especially with respect to morality. "The quality of being that constitutes a criminal cannot be clearly known," he wrote, "until observed as belonging to the class from which criminals come." Moreover, "to reduce crime a true prison system should recognize the criminal classes for what they are and bring to bear upon them the forces necessary to modify their behavior."

The height of the excitement about (and the brightest hopes for) reformatories occurred in the 1870s and 1880s, when numerous state and federal reformatories were built. By 1888, every effort was made by reformatory officials to estimate the rate of recidivism among the 1,722 inmates paroled since the opening of the reformatory in 1876 through September 30, 1887. Inquiries were sent to every paroled prisoner—wherever he might be—and to his relatives, employers, and/or acquaintances. Definite information was obtained on 1,125 former prisoners. The board of managers proudly declared that the public enjoyed protection to the extent of "90 percent" of the whole number received and treated, and, in regard to men paroled, over 80 percent were considered as "probable reformations." To the extent that these statistics were accurate, they would indicate an extraordinarily low cumulative recidivism rate of 10 percent for the first 11 years of the existence of the reformatory. That success was further expressed in the statement that more than 80 percent were paroled after having served a little over one year within the reformatory and later went on to establish themselves as right-living, law-abiding citizens.

Although by 1890 the population at the reformatory had exceeded the limits outlined by the first planning commission (500 was the original population limit), there had been some modification of the general scheme of treatment of the "patients." Nevertheless, there had been a specialization of function and a singleness of direction. Moral, mental, and manual training had been systematically coordinated with the end in view of producing practical, self-helping, and self-governing citizens.

The Elmira Reformatory was the source of numerous innovations in offender treatment and prison management. The following is a brief description of the major innovations in penology pioneered at Elmira:

**Young First-time Offenders.** It was believed when Elmira was established that if young first-time offenders were segregated from older, more hardened criminals, then reformation was more probable.

**The Indeterminate Sentence and Inmate Treatment.** Comparing crime to a disease, it was believed that the patient should be kept under treatment until cured. Thus, the indeterminate sentence was established as a basic principle. The reformatory prescription consisted of a trinity of "Ms"—mental, moral, and manual training.

**A Progressive Stage System of Classification.** Inmates at the reformatory were classified into three grades (designated as the "first," "second," and "third") until 1890, when the grades changed in name. Movement up and down the grading system was determined by the number of marks a prisoner earned each month.

**The Marking System.** Designed by Maconochie and carried out in Ireland by Crofton, the mark system provided an incentive for hard work and good conduct. It also kept intact some of the economic motives available in free society, introducing a wage system at Elmira.

**Parole.** Parole was based on the mark system, which indicated the progress of the men in preparation for discharge. In 1890, no system of prison discipline other than Elmira included such an elaborate plan of official oversight of paroled men. From Elmira, paroled men were sent to the care of an agent of the reformatory in the city or town in which they had secured employment.

**The Physical Culture Program.** As a major form of treatment at the reformatory, the physical culture program (for "dullards and weaklings") was regarded as an effective way to treat even the most unpromising of prisoners. As such, it represents the first attempt in US prison history to emphasize exercise, diet, and general physical fitness as important factors in the reduction of criminal tendencies in young adult felons.

**Military Drill Program.** A direct result of the Yates Act of 1888 that ended all prison labor for profit, the inmates were organized into a military battalions, substituting drilling for daily labor. So firmly had the military regime been established that even when the trades school was reorganized and means were found for reestablishing prison industries, it remained undisturbed.

**School of Letters.** The signature of a reformatory system of prison discipline, the educational program, was established at Elmira in 1877. Attendance then, as ever, was compulsory. The course of study increased year by year in efficiency and grew wider in range until, by 1890, it was bounded by a kindergarten on one hand and a college curriculum on the other. Over time, the reformatory was referred to as "the college on the hill."

**Moral Education.** In addition to religious services, certain courses in ethics, sociology, and political science were intended to help the prisoner form his ideals and his conduct. Moral training at the reformatory was constant. In their everyday interaction with one another and with the officials, the inmates were impressed with the advantages of doing right through unremitting practice of right behavior.

**Trades School Training.** Systematic trade training began in 1886, based upon the discovery that most of the prisoners had no trade. Three connected, one-story pavilions were equipped with the necessary items for teaching the basics of half a dozen trades. Two nights of every week, 120 men attended classes for an hour and a half. The ability to earn a living at some recognized trade was nearly indispensable to conditional release by 1890.

**The Prison Library.** Nearly half of the library containing the educational and scientific works was reserved for the reference of those pursuing special branches of study. The other books were distributed to the inmates in their cells according to their assignment in one of the three grades.

**The Prison Newspaper.** The *Summary* must be regarded as a pioneer among prison newspapers. The first of its kind, it made its initial appearance in 1883. By 1890, it had been printed and circulated among the inmates and their friends every Sunday morning without interruption.

**Organized Sports.** Elmira was the first correctional institution to use games such as baseball, basketball, football, and track-and-field as "treatment" rather than mere diversion.

**Prison Labor.** Several manufacturing industries at the reformatory were introduced in order to meet the capabilities of the prisoners. When duly trained, prisoners were paid wages by the piece, process, or by the hour at a rate equal to the lowest regular wages paid to free laborers for similar work and service.

Contemporary calls for a reformatory system of prison discipline must not confuse reform with rehabilitation and/or deterrence, a problem that has and will continue to have serious consequences for correctional practice. The architects of the Elmira Reformatory eschewed vindictive punishment as counterproductive and would have objected to the vague, often meaningless treatment programs designed to rehabilitate offenders in the 1960s and 1970s. The Elmira system was not punitive by design and was very explicit in terms of what was expected from offenders. It is possible that if replicated (with modifications), the Elmira system would be infinitely superior to contemporary correctional practice, which is too often a mixture of three very different and conflicting correctional rationales.

# One

# Reform and the Elmira Reformatory

The initial step taken towards the establishment of the Elmira Reformatory was the creation in 1869 by the New York State Legislature of a commission "to locate a State penitentiary or industrial reformatory in the Sixth Judicial District." The report of this body contracting for the present site was definitely acted upon in the following year, when a board of five commissioners was authorized and the work of construction was begun. The building commissioners were legislated out of office in 1874, their duties being assigned to a superintending builder. Only a portion of the main structure had been completed, and $700,000 had been spent when, on May 9, 1876, the legislature passed an act providing a government for the embryo institution, and the superintending builder was succeeded by the board of managers. The first inmates were received on July 24, 1876, after being transferred from Auburn prison. Thereafter, the prisoners carried on most of the construction work. The institution did not take its distinctive position in the prison system of the state, however, until April 24, 1877, when the bill providing for the indeterminate sentence was incorporated in the statutes. By 1888, the success of the treatment program was such that the reformatory had, after 12 years, firmly established itself as something more than an experiment. Some of the early advocates of reform are identified in the following pages.

The earliest advocate for reform of the US prison system, and for the "moral reform" of prisoners, was Edward Livingston (1764–1836). His position was clearly stated in his Code of Reform and Prison Discipline in 1824. The true object of punishment should be the protection of society through the prevention of crime and reformation of the criminal. Reformation was the transformation of the morally corrupt into acceptable responsible citizens.

The principles of the indeterminate sentence (or indefinite sentence, as it was originally conceived) and, ultimately, parole were first announced in 1839 by Frederic Hill (1803–1896) in one of his reports as government inspector of prisons for Scotland. Hill likened the treatment of a criminal to that of a madman who no one would think of releasing until deemed "cured."

Capt. Alexander Maconochie (1787–1860) of the Royal Navy was put in charge of the penal colony on Norfolk Island from 1840 to 1844 (after serving as secretary to the governor of New South Wales). He recommended that sentences to a fixed period of imprisonment should be replaced by sentences to a fixed amount of labor. This he proposed to measure by marks, hence the name given to his system. In 1854, Sir Walter Crofton (1815–1897) based his system of convict discipline upon Captain Maconochie's plan. The Irish System was devised and inaugurated in Ireland from 1854 to 1862. Crofton introduced, besides reformatory treatment, a four-stage graduated release component. The first stage was severely penal, with nine months in solitary. In the second stage, the prisoner was permitted to work with other inmates and to earn marks to progress to the third stage. In the third stage, the prisoner was sent to an open institution where he could earn his release on a ticket of leave. In the fourth stage, the inmate was released from custody and supervised on the outside by the police.

The notion that criminals were the victims of factors beyond their control was a departure from the 18th-century free choice theory of crime. According to E.C. Wines (1806–1879), the requirements for the reformation of prisoners were believed to be as follows: a strong desire on the part of prison officers to accomplish this result and a conviction that prisoners were capable of being reformed; individualized treatment that sought to gain the will and not merely to coerce the body; an indefinite sentence to run until the prisoner was reformed (this was of vital importance because a criminal was a man who was morally diseased and in need of a "cure"); religious instruction because of its potential to transform the human life and spirit; education that offered opportunities for social and personal improvement; productive labor; and vigilant oversight to prevent the abuse of power on the part of reformatory officials. As secretary of the Prison Association of New York, Dr. Wines was very influential in the passage of the law establishing the Elmira Reformatory.

Theodore W. Dwight (1822–1892) was a noted lawyer and educator with a long history of concern for prisons and the treatment of prisoners. Significantly, he was one of the five commissioners who selected Elmira as the most suitable location for the new reformatory. An early expression of the need for prison reform and a reformatory system of prison discipline is found in "Report on the Prisons and Reformatories of the United States and Canada" by Dr. Enoch Cobb Wines and Theodore W. Dwight (published in 1867). The most critical finding of their extensive examination of state prisons in the United States was that not one of them was seeking the reformation of its inmates as a primary object. Their recommendation was the adoption of the Irish System of prison discipline for New York's state prison apparatus. This conclusion was instrumental in the organization of the National Congress on Penitentiary and Reformatory Discipline, held in Cincinnati in 1870.

Dr. Hamilton D. Wey was born in Wilkes-Barre, Pennsylvania, on July 29, 1854. He served as chief medical officer of the reformatory from 1879 to 1900. Beginning with his experimental group in 1886, Wey was responsible for the establishment of the physical culture program at the reformatory. It was under his direction and with Brockway's enthusiastic support that the reformatory moved from moral and intellectual reform to pathological reform. The transition was clear in the *1892 Annual Report of the Board of Managers*, which contains numerous pictures of prisoners with various so-called physical defects indicative of criminal propensities. By 1887, physical training continued upon the general plan described in Dr. Wey's 1886 report. He subjected 31 men who were dullards and physically deficient to his treatment. A sufficient number responded to this method of treatment to demonstrate the value of the bodily training as an educational measure in the care of the criminal dullard. In February 1900, the senior physician, H.D. Wey, MD, tendered his resignation at the request of the board of managers of the Elmira Reformatory.

Zebulon Brockway (1827–1920) began his 50 years of prison employment in 1848 as a clerk at the Wethersfield State Prison in Connecticut. In 1869, a reformatory was authorized in the state of New York to receive male offenders between the ages of 16 and 30. The following year, the first convention of the American Prison Association met in Cincinnati. At the 1870 convention, famously known as the National Congress on Penitentiary and Reformatory Discipline, Zebulon Brockway presented a paper based on the Irish System that dealt with the idea of an indeterminate sentence and the possibilities of a system of parole. The prison reformers meeting in Cincinnati urged New York to adopt Brockway's proposal at Elmira. When the Elmira Reformatory opened in 1876, Brockway was appointed superintendent. For Brockway, the causes of crime were to be found in class differences, especially with respect to morality. "The quality of being that constitutes a criminal cannot be clearly known," he wrote, "until observed as belonging to the class from which criminals come." Moreover, a true prison system should recognize the criminal classes and bring to bear upon them the forces necessary to modify their behavior.

Under the authority of chapter 427 of the laws of 1870 (passed on April 27, 1870), Gov. John T. Hoffman (1828–1888; pictured at left) appointed the following as building commissioners for the erection of the state prison (or industrial reformatory established at Elmira in Chemung County): Amos Pilsbury of Albany, Charles B. Walker of Corning, Abram H. Miller of Oswego, Stephen T. Arnot of Elmira, and Frank H. Atkinson of Elmira.

William L. Woollett (1815–1874), the architect-in-chief, was an Englishman who immigrated to Albany. He drew up the plans for the Elmira Reformatory in 1871, according to the ideas of Amos Pilsbury.

# *Two*

# The Physical Plant of the Reformatory

On April 29, 1869, Gov. John T. Hoffman signed chapter 408 of the laws of 1869 into effect. The act provided that five commissioners appointed by the governor select a site upon which to erect a state penitentiary or industrial reformatory. Dr. Theodore W. Dwight was one of the five commissioners who selected Elmira as the most suitable location for the new reformatory. In their opinion, the best method was to treat a young class of criminals between the ages of 16 and 30. "We thought it better," said Dr. Dwight, "to take only those sentenced for their first offence. Our idea then was to bring to bear on them reformatory influences—reformatory as distinguished from penal. We adopted the main thought of Crofton's Irish System, namely to commence a course of discipline with strictly solitary confinement." Amos Pilsbury, a member of the first building commission, prepared the preliminary and working plans for the reformatory. Architect J.F. Bryant was employed to draft preliminary plans embodying commissioner Pilbury's ideas with reference to the proposed reformatory. The governor of New York approved the architectural plans for the new reformatory submitted by William L. Woollett on January 25, 1871. The reformatory was not to be a place constructed solely for the incarceration of individuals convicted of crime. Thus, it was necessary to provide the means for gradation and separation among the convicts in the design of the facility itself. That was exactly what Woollett's design was meant to provide. By the spring of 1876, when the first board of managers of the reformatory replaced the building commission, more than $700,000 had already been spent on construction of the new facility. Four large factories were built in 1879, and other necessary buildings were added every year after. In 1889, the new physical training building was in full progress, the chapel was enlarged, and operations in connection with the new north wing extension were well under way. Out of 280 acres belonging to the reformatory, the prison enclosure occupied only 14. The total outlay of funds for the entire reformatory project was, by 1890, close to $2 million.

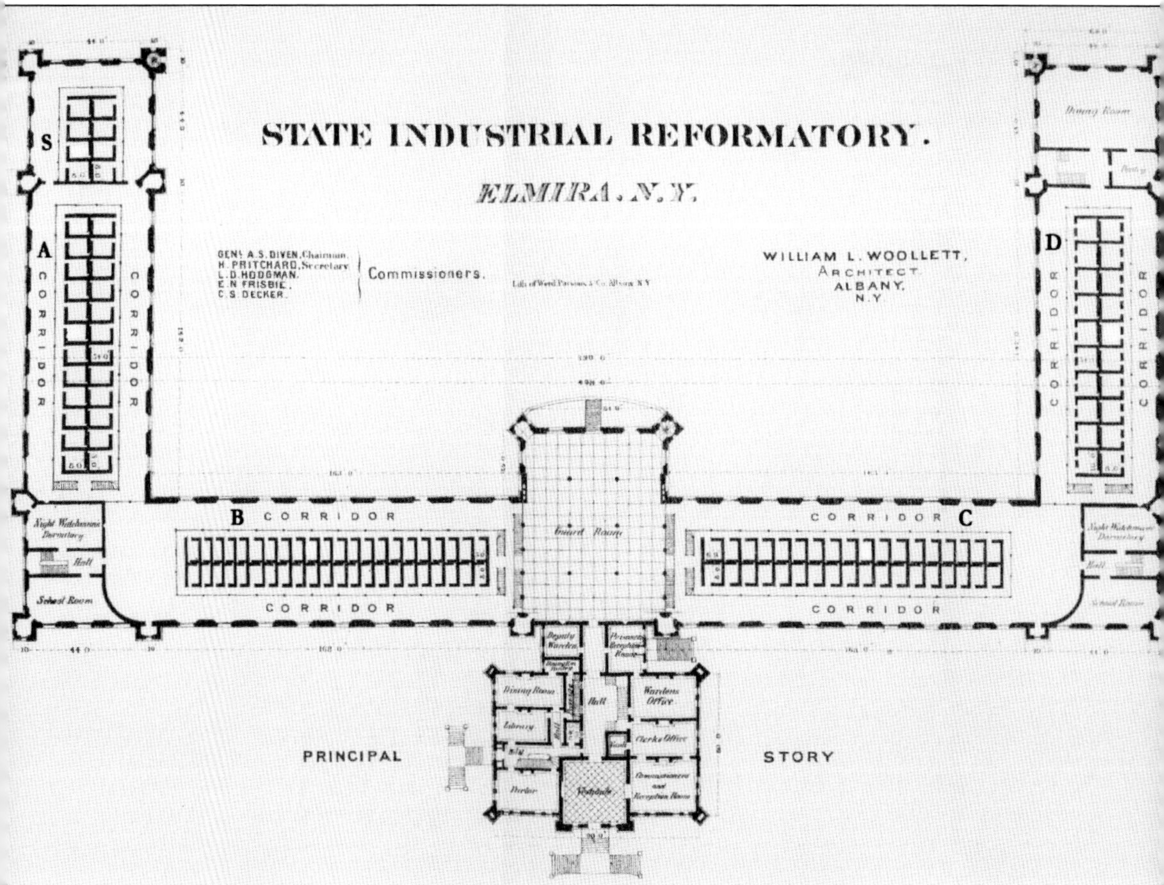


According to Woollett, his 1871 plan was an entirely new thing in prison architecture: "It was an attempt to carry out Crofton's 'Irish System' beneath one roof; never attempted before." Prisoners would be received in the second grade and housed in either cell block B or C. Once promoted to the first grade, prisoners would move to cell block D. Third-grade prisoners were housed in south wing A or in seclusion unit S for punishment.

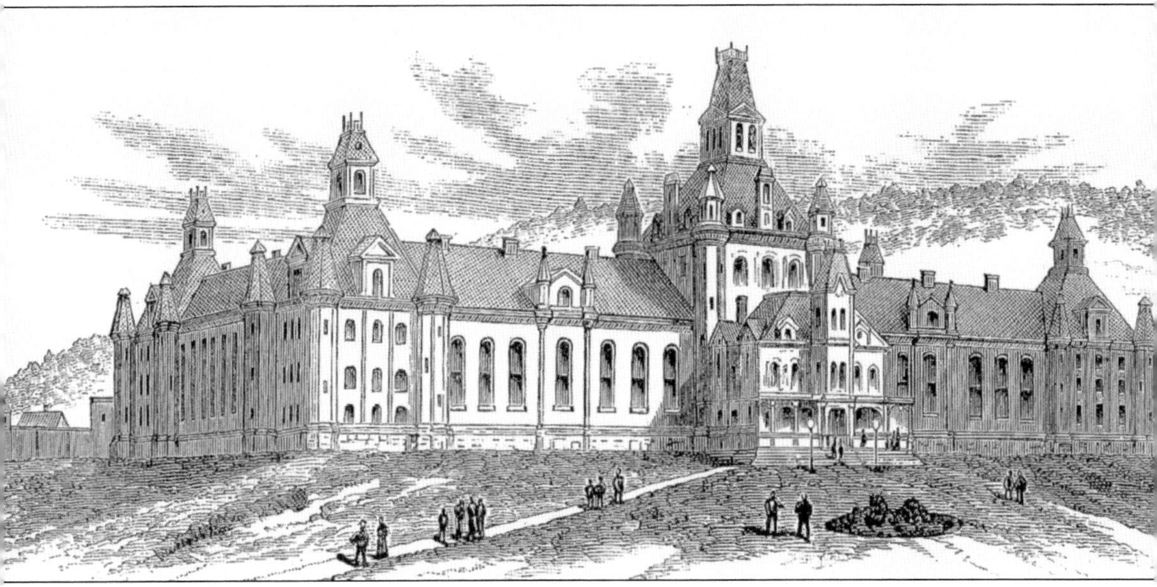

Hidden from view in this 1886 sketch of the reformatory are the north wing, the northwest pavilion, the center wall between the eastern or front prison yard, and the western or back prison yard. Directly behind the main entrance and warden's residence, the central feature was the three-story administration building, above which was a columned cupola. In this photograph, people are seen walking away from the front entrance of the warden's residence.

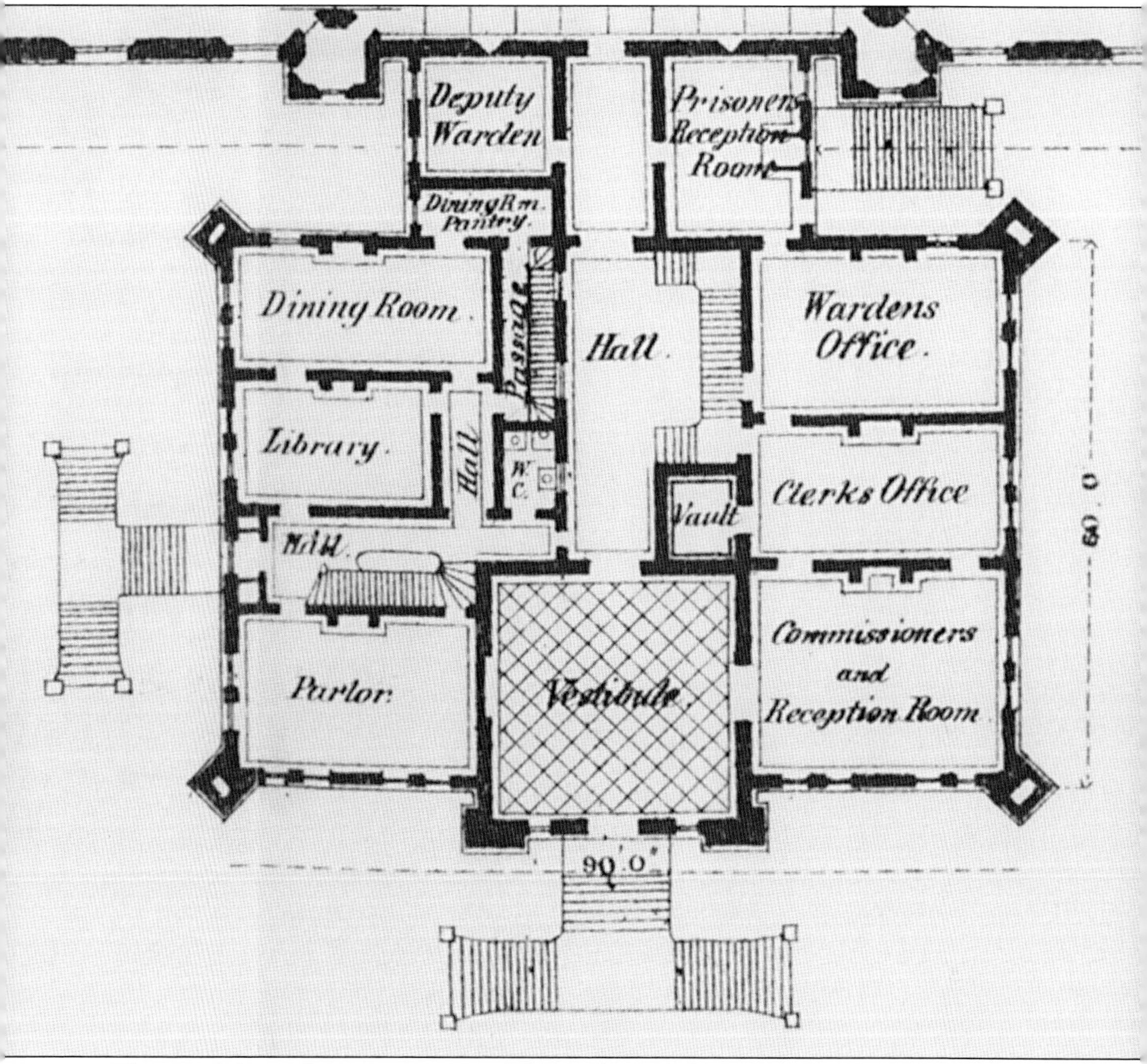


This detail shows the various rooms of the warden's residence. It was the main entrance to the reformatory proper, located in front of the guardroom and connected to it by a narrow passage.

From the very beginning, construction work on the reformatory had been conducted in a manner so unsatisfactory that on May 5, 1874, the legislature abolished the building commission and authorized Gov. John A. Dix to appoint a superintending builder. The governor appointed John R. Thomas (1848–1901) of Rochester, New York, architect and sole commissioner for the erection of the state reformatory at Elmira under chapter 323 of the laws of 1874.

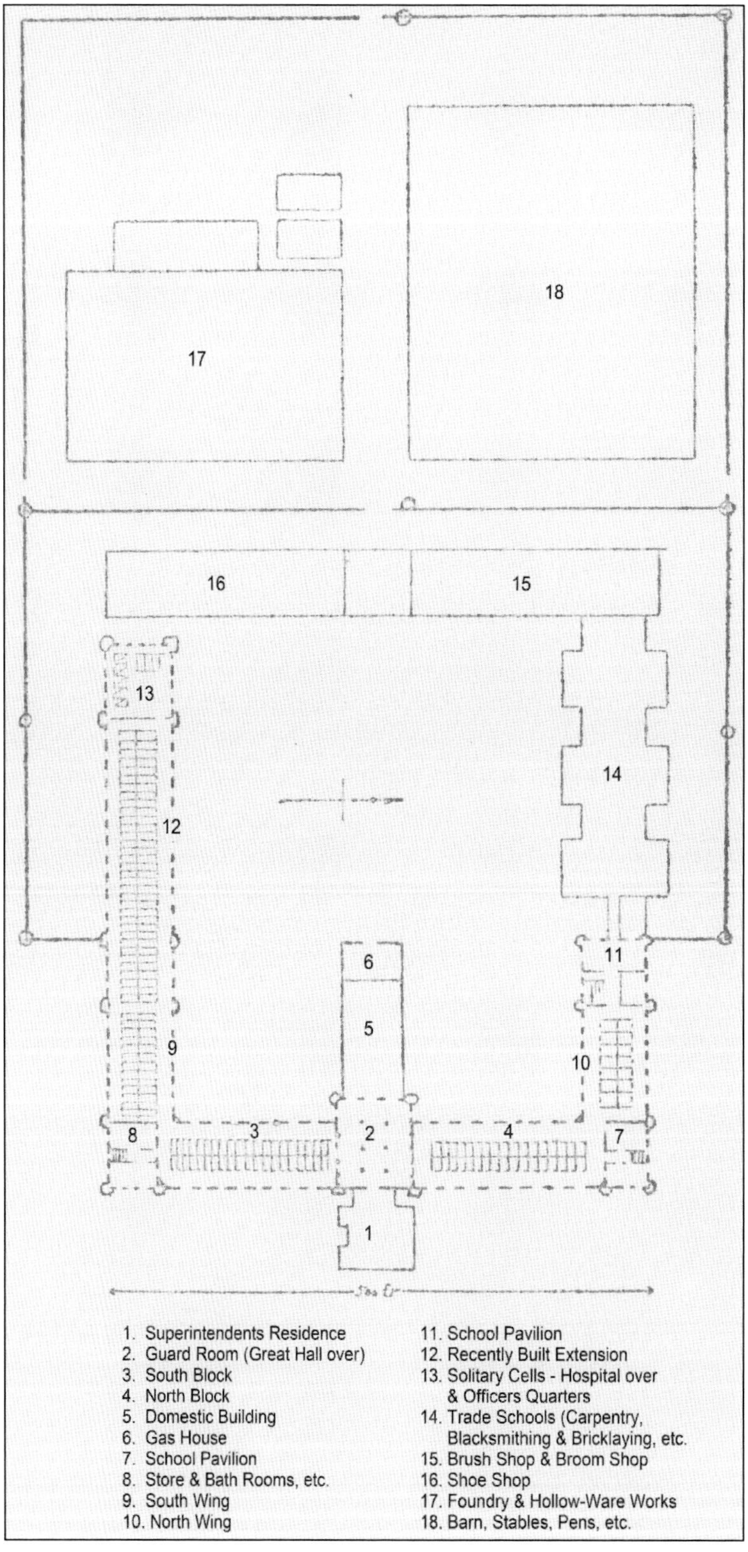


This is the first floor plan of the reformatory published. Found in a booklet published by the board of managers in 1886 titled *Papers in Penology*, it was meant to give the public a better understanding of what the reformatory was attempting to accomplish. Included in the legend are the superintendents residence and guard room (great hall over).

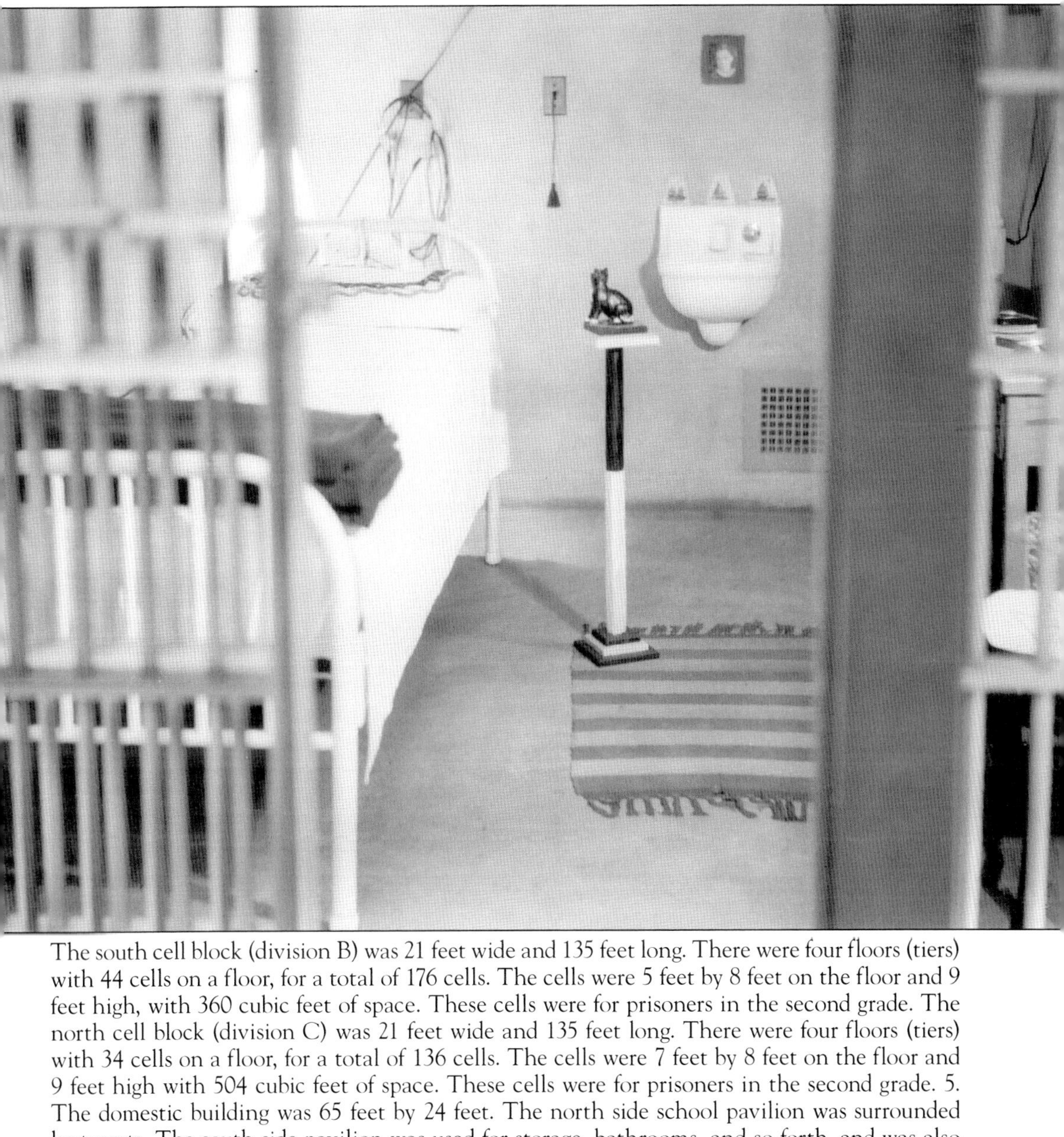

The south cell block (division B) was 21 feet wide and 135 feet long. There were four floors (tiers) with 44 cells on a floor, for a total of 176 cells. The cells were 5 feet by 8 feet on the floor and 9 feet high, with 360 cubic feet of space. These cells were for prisoners in the second grade. The north cell block (division C) was 21 feet wide and 135 feet long. There were four floors (tiers) with 34 cells on a floor, for a total of 136 cells. The cells were 7 feet by 8 feet on the floor and 9 feet high with 504 cubic feet of space. These cells were for prisoners in the second grade. 5. The domestic building was 65 feet by 24 feet. The north side school pavilion was surrounded by turrets. The south side pavilion was used for storage, bathrooms, and so forth, and was also surrounded by turrets. Pictured above is a cell in the south cell block.

The south wing cell block (division A) was 21 feet wide and 234 feet long. There were four floors with 26 cells on a floor, for a total of 104 cells. The cells were 5 feet by 8 feet on the floor and 9 feet high, with 360 cubic feet of space. These cells were for prisoners in the third grade. The north wing cell block (division D) was 21 feet by 77 feet. There were four floors (tiers) with 14 cells on a floor, for a total of 56 cells. The cells were 8 feet by 10 feet on the floor and 9 feet high, containing 720 cubic feet of space. These cells were for the privileged class of prisoners in the first grade. The north side school pavilion was surrounded by turrets. Pictured above is the south wing cell block.

The south side solitary cells pavilion (division S) was also surrounded by turrets. There were four floors (tiers) with 8 cells on a floor, for a total of 32 cells. The cells were 8 feet square on the floor and 9 feet high with 576 cubic feet of space. The north side trades school building contained work spaces for carpentry, blacksmithing, bricklaying, and so forth. Pictured above is the south side solitary pavilion.

In 1891, there were 280 acres of land contained in the reformatory property, of which only about 15 acres were enclosed. The outlying portion was tilled, producing food for the livestock and garden vegetables for consumption by prisoners and staff at the institution. The enclosure occupied a small plateau on a hill. Over time, the reformatory came to be called "the college on the hill," in recognition of its extensive educational program. On the west side of the Chemung Valley, the reformatory was 2.5 miles from the post office of Elmira and within the city boundaries. The main building formed its eastern front, which was more than 650 feet long. It was constructed of brick and trimmed with blue stone. The facade, which was quite ornate and architecturally novel for a building of the kind, was painted a steel gray. The style chosen was, according to the building commissioners, "a modification of the Italian with a tree treatment, to the end that it should present at once a chaste and dignified exterior as well as a massive one, and also do away with the cold, repellant appearance of a prison."

On either side of the three-story administration building, cell houses extended to four-story octagon pavilions, whose corners were surmounted by slender towers. In front of the guard room, connected to it by a narrow passage, was the main entrance to the reformatory itself. It was also the residence of the general superintendent. On the first floor was the office of the chief clerk and the cashier. From the southeast pavilion, which contained bathrooms, quartermasters' office, supply rooms, and officers' apartments, a cell house (the south wing) extended to the west about 300 feet. From the northeast pavilion, used for schoolrooms and officers' quarters, another cell house (the north wing) extended to the west about 250 feet. Both these structures terminated in pavilions, similar in form to those in the front. The pavilion on the southwest side included in its five floors the seclusion (punishment) cells, storerooms, employees' quarters, and the hospital. The pavilion on the northwest side was reserved chiefly for classrooms. The pavilion of the 1891 north wing extension can be seen at the extreme right of this photograph.

North of both wings, there was still another cell house (which was also parallel to both wings) 500 feet in length. The cell house connected with the main building at the north pavilion. This wing was constructed in 1891 and would be occupied by that winter. The legislature of 1890 made an appropriation for the north wing extension (pictured above), which, when completed, added 504 new cells, thus raising the capacity of the institution to 1,200.

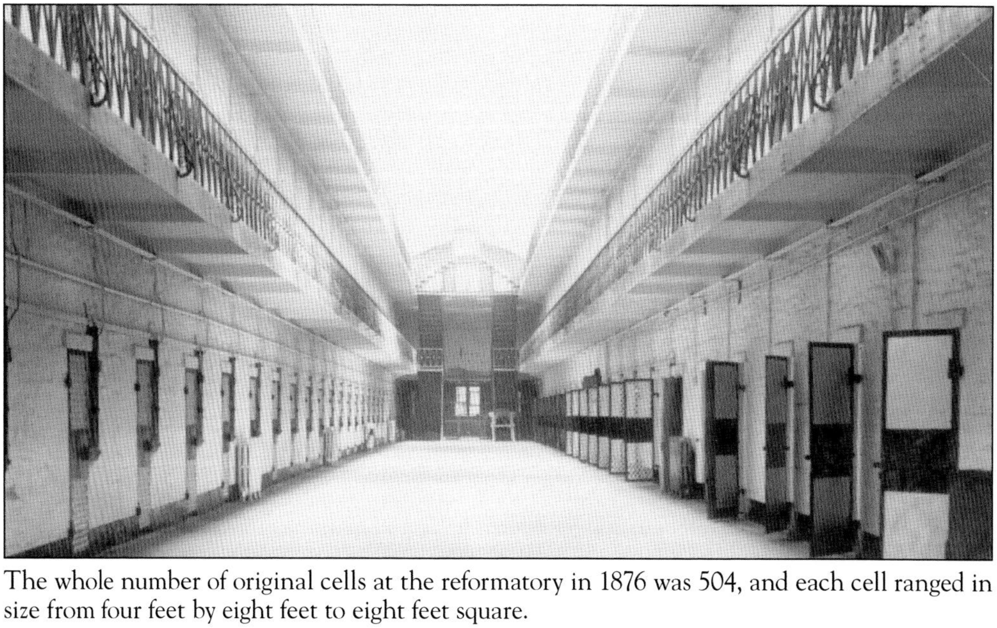

The whole number of original cells at the reformatory in 1876 was 504, and each cell ranged in size from four feet by eight feet to eight feet square.

Directly in the rear of (and adjoining) the central building was the domestic building. This brick structure, about 250 feet by 50 feet, housed a baking plant capable of turning out 2,000 loaves of bread a day in the basement. By 1891, the ground floor of the domestic building (see floor plan and key Nos. 25–35) was occupied by, among other things, the employee and inmate kitchens, the tailor shop, zinc etching and photography workrooms, the laundry and drying room (and soap vats), the baking and culinary department, the dining room for the farm laborers, the meat room, the ice room, the general storeroom for comestibles, and the engine and dynamo room. A feature of this floor was the receiving room for new arrivals. This room was furnished both with bathtubs and the requisite instruments of measurements for identification purposes. The area in the foreground, where a man is seen walking, was the parade ground for the military drill program. Note the dummy artillery in the bottom left corner of the photograph.

By September 30, 1890, the population at the reformatory had reached 1,102, far exceeding the limits outlined by the first planning commission (500 was the original population limit), and there had been some modification of the general scheme of treatment of the patients.

# New York State Reformatory.

**Extreme Length of Enclosure, 1148 ft. Extreme Width of Enclosure, 740 ft.**
**Enclosure contains 15 Acres.**

Cost of Plant, in Round Numbers, $1,800,000

## *Key to Ground Plan.*

1. BOILER ROOMS.
2. ENGINE ROOMS.
3. DRYING ROOMS.
4. OFFICES.
5. FOUNDRY CUPOLA.
6. STORE ROOMS.
7. MILLING ROOM.
8. MODEL ROOM.
9. BATH HOUSE.
10. JAPANNING ROOM.
11. BUCKET HOUSE.
12. GREEN HOUSE.
13. OIL HOUSE.
14. HOSE DRYING TOWER.
15. TEAMSTERS' ROOMS.
16. CARRIAGE ROOM.
17. FIRE ENGINE ROOM.
18. PAINT ROOM.
19. STORE ROOM.
20. CENTRE GATE.
21. SOUTH WING PAVILION.
22. STORE ROOM.
23. BATH ROOM.
24. ADMINISTRATION BUILDING.
25. AUXILIARY DYNAMO ROOM.
26. MEAT COOLING ROOMS.
27. PRISON KITCHEN.
28. PROVISION ROOM.
29. OFFICERS' KITCHEN.
30. OFFICERS' DINING ROOM.
31. LAUNDRY DRY ROOM.
32. TAILOR SHOP.
33. OFFICERS' LAUNDRY.
34. PRISON LAUNDRY.
35. PHOTOGRAPH GALLERY.
36. GYMNASIUM, PLUNGE BATH.
37. GYMNASIUM, SINKS.
38. GYMNASIUM, DRESSING ROOM.
39. GYMNASIUM, SHAMPOOING ROOM.
40. GYMNASIUM, WARM AND HOT ROOMS
41. DYNAMO HOUSE.
42. NORTH WING PAVILION.
43. SCHOOL ROOMS.
44. GENERAL SUPERINTENDENT'S RESIDENCE.

## *Trades Class Rooms.*

(*Ground floor only.*)

A. WOOD WORKING MACHINERY.
B. CABINET MAKING.
C. WOOD CARVING.
D. SHOE MAKING.
E. IRON MOULDING.
F. BRASS FINISHING.
G. BRASS MOULDING.
H. HARDWARE FINISHING.
I. WOOD TURNING.
J. STEAM FITTING
K. CARPENTRY.
L. PATTERN MAKING.
M. TINSMITHING.
N. MACHINISTS.
O. HORSE-SHOEING.
P. IRON FORGING.
Q. PLUMBING.
R. BRICK-LAYING.
S. PLASTERING.
T. FRESCOING.

In the *1891 Annual Report of the Board of Managers*, a full floor plan, seen on the following page, with a key, above, is provided.

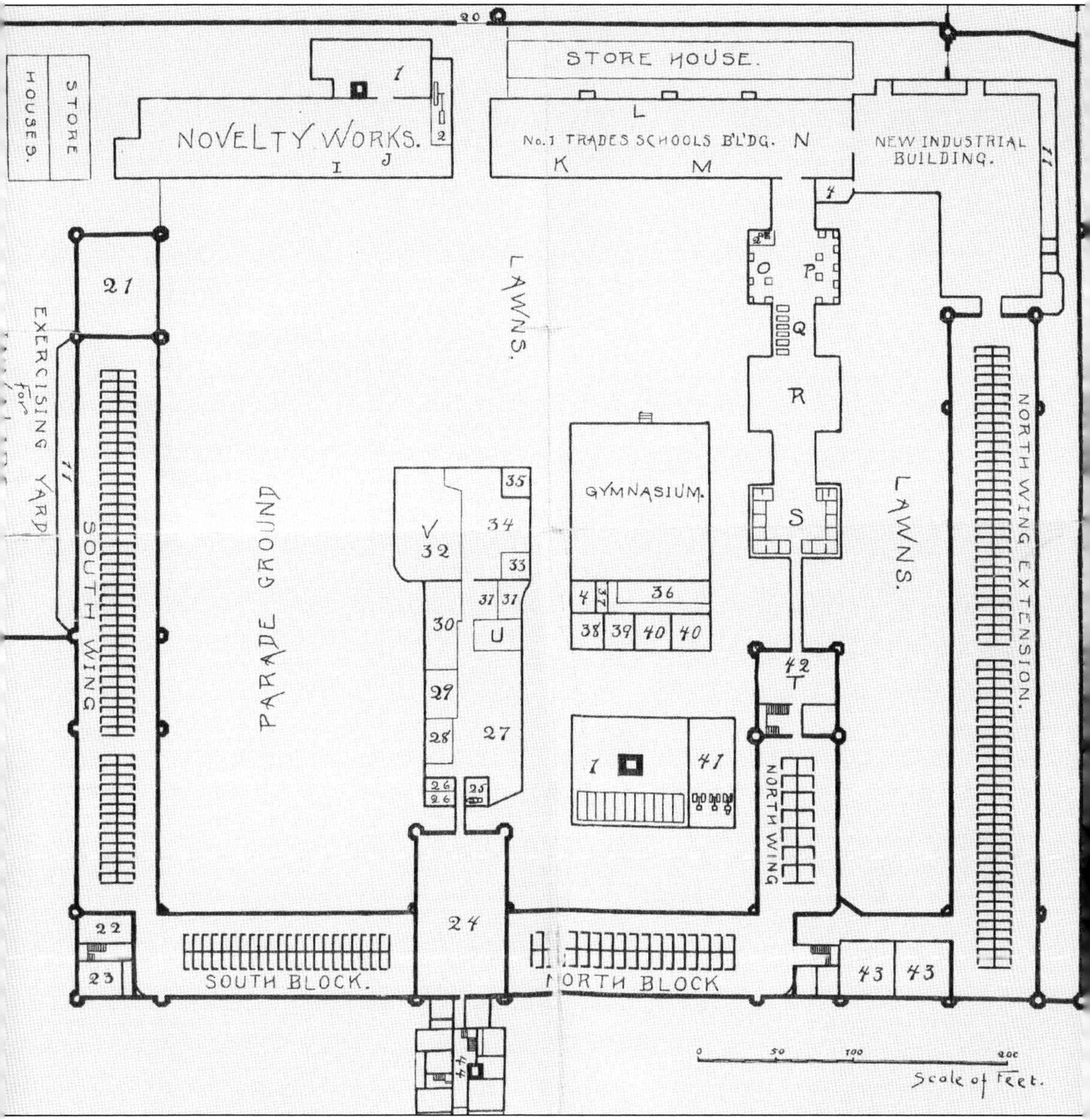


A stone-capped brick wall 20 feet high bound the three sides of the 15 acres of enclosure in the rear of the main building. At suitable intervals were sentry houses for guards during inclement weather. Guards patrolled the walls during the working hours of the day and when inmates were out of the cell houses and their immediate annexes. Halfway between the administration building (No. 24) and the rear guard wall (overlooking the western or back yard), there was another wall paralleling them that divided the enclosure into two nearly equal parts (east and west yards). The eastern yard (pictured above) contained (aside from the north and south wings or cell blocks of the front structure) a series of three connecting, one-story, Greek cross–shaped pavilions, in which the newly established trades school was located. There was also a two-story, 500-foot-by-50-foot factory structure known as No. 1 trade school and a new three-story, 260-foot-by-50 foot industrial building that was soon to be occupied. The greater portion of floor space of these buildings was given to the trades school classes.

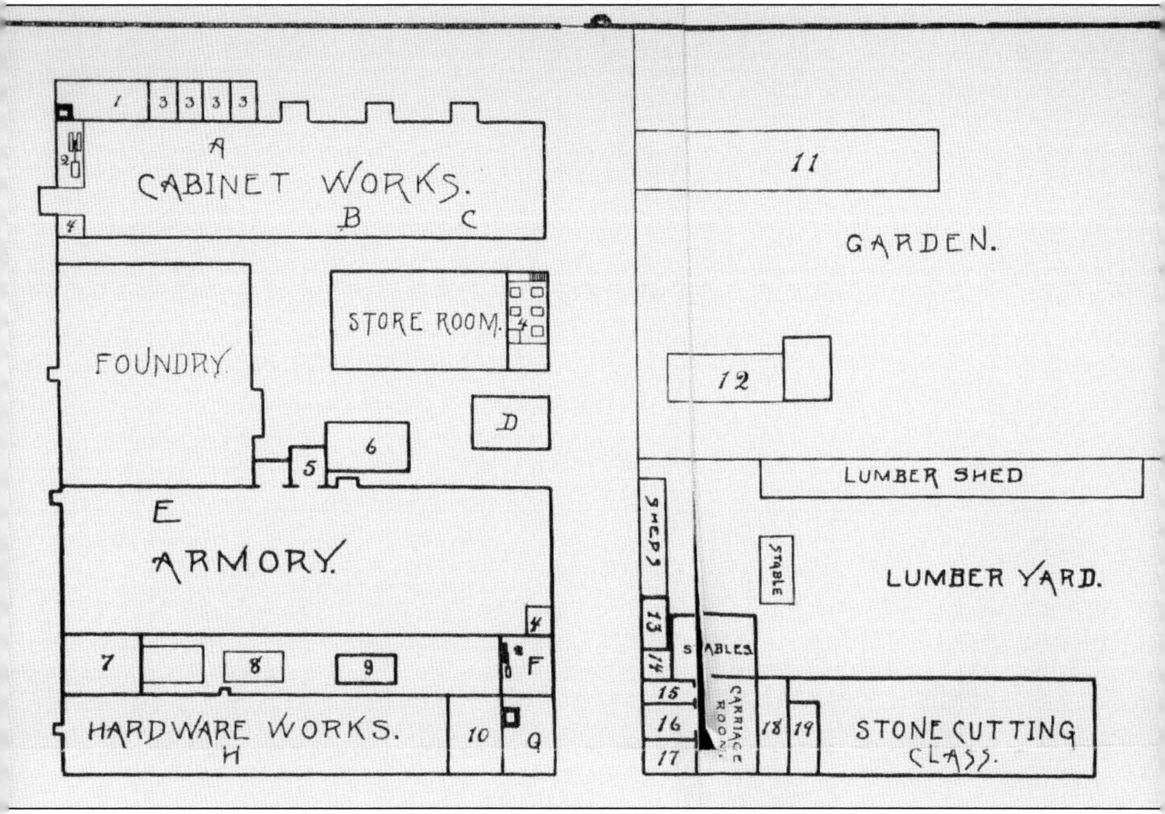


In the eastern yard—located next to the exercising yard for invalids on the south side and behind the new industrial building on the north side—were the so-called "bucket houses." These were for the disposal of human waste from the night buckets that prisoners had in their cells (there was no indoor plumbing in 1891). In the west yard were the hardware, brass-working, cabinet and upholstery, boat building, stone-cutting, and shoe shop areas; the iron foundry; armory; inside business office; stables for carriage horses and light vehicles; a shelter for a steam fire engine and hose carriage; an ice house; storehouses; and a limited garden patch.

The only access between the east and west yards was by means of an opening in the center dividing wall. At this pass, designated the center gate, an officer was constantly stationed during daily business hours. From his vantage point, he commanded a view of the three gates that opened to outside roads leading in as many directions, and all loads moving in either direction had to be carefully scrutinized and recorded by him. His presence was also a check on a too-free circulation of inmates about the shops, since none of the inmates were permitted to go from one side of the arch to the other without a pass signed by someone in authority.

In close proximity to the southern wall were capacious grain and stock barns, the latter containing the draught animals required for moving freight to and from the railways and for other heavy hauling.

In the summertime, the number of men employed on the reformatory acres was about 15. In the winter, the number was gradually reduced, as there was always some work to be done about the barn and stables.

The farm barns were located outside the enclosure. The men selected to work in the fields and around these buildings were those nearer the probability of their parole. In 1891, there were 20 cows and 200 swine on the premises.

For building operations, the stock of 25 horses was used in heavy work. Some were used for errand purposes in order to keep up communication between the reformatory and the city of Elmira.

The horses were also used to pull the fire engine located in the firehouse, inside the walls of the reformatory, when required.

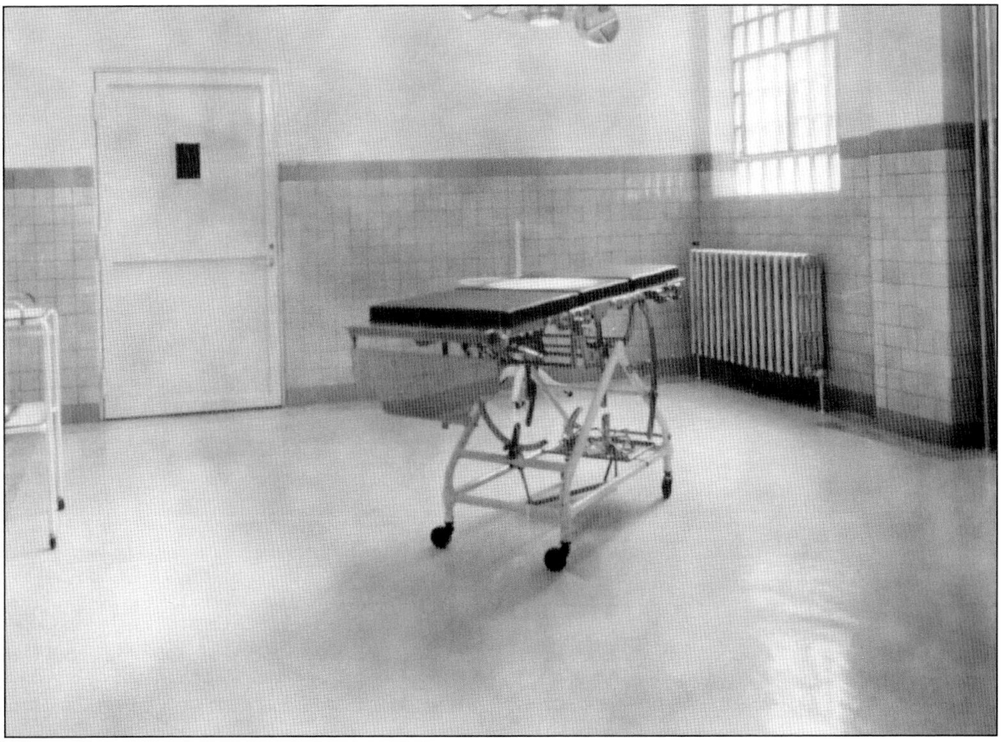

The southwest wing pavilion (No. 21 on the floor plan on page 33) included the hospital. In 1891, the hospital was reached by a large elevator and was at all times kept scrupulously neat, clean, and perfectly supplied with all manner of appliances for any sort of sickness or casualty.

Men were not taken to the hospital upon slight pretexts. However, whenever a real case of need for special treatment developed, there was no hesitation on the part of those in authority to have the man transferred to the hospital (pending a decision by the physician).

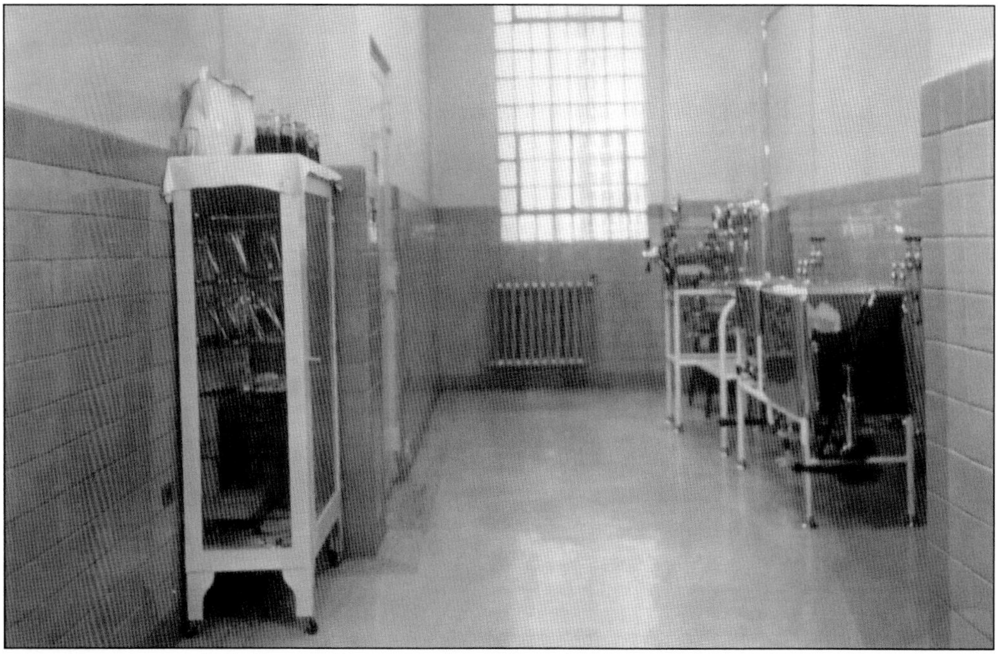

The physician made daily rounds among the sick and maintained careful supervision over all who were under hospital treatment.

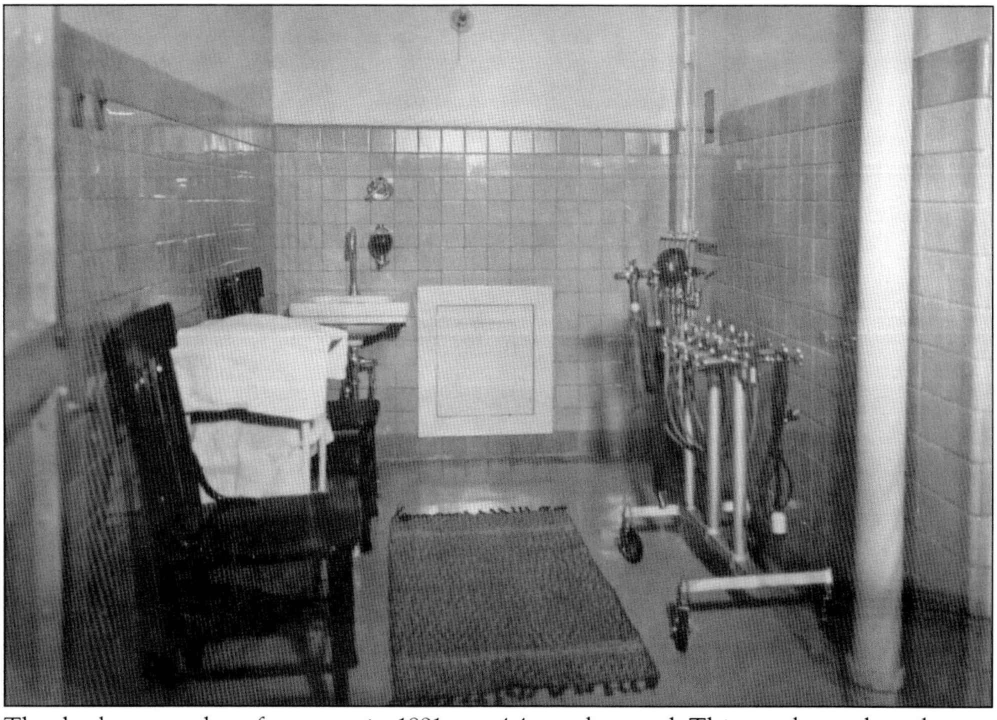

The death rate at the reformatory in 1891 was 4.4 per thousand. This was lower than the city of Elmira, no doubt due to the systematized work of the institution in every department. The regular diet, the even distribution of time allotted to work, study, and rest, and the freedom from excesses of all kinds had a marked effect in this regard.

Underneath the hospital were the dormitories and general rooms of the officers (No. 21 on the floor plan on page 33). The same degree of order and neatness required of the inmates was required of the officers. The officers' quarters included baths, reading rooms, and recreation rooms. These were intended to supply, in some measure, something akin to homelike features in the life of those who made their home voluntarily within the walls of the institution. A few senior officers were accommodated in quarters at the extremities of the north and south blocks.

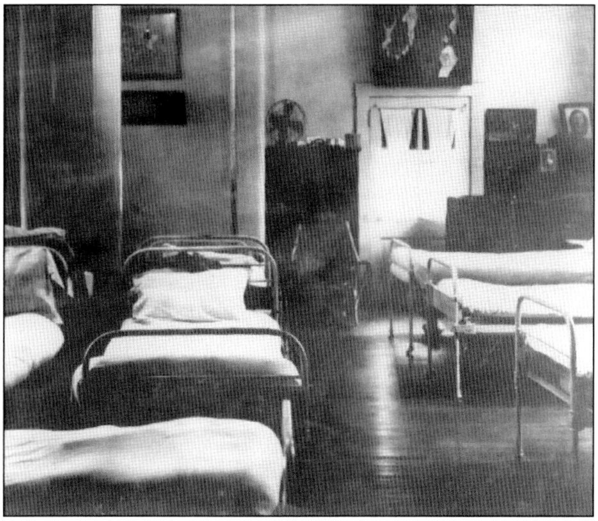

For many years, the reformatory was lighted by gas manufactured on the premises. By 1890, a system of electric lighting was in operation. A building was erected to house four dynamos, which were run by two 120-horsepower engines. It appears on the 1891 floor plan on pages 32–33 as the "dynamo house" (No. 41). A competent electrician was engaged to take care of it, and the system developed so that 1,700 incandescent lights and 35 arc lights were in use.

The hallways and classrooms were all freely illuminated by incandescent lights, and there was a light of this kind in each cell throughout the entire establishment. These lights were turned off at half past nine, except in rooms where men in the upper-first grade had earned the privilege to burn a "late-light" for purposes of study. The use of the electric light gave a "comfortable and cozy appearance" to the rooms in the evening, and the use of the arc lights on the exterior of the buildings constituted a prominent feature in the night landscape.

The meals for nearly 1,500 people were all prepared in the domestic building. The basement included a large kitchen in which inmates' soups, stews, and hash were prepared in great steam-heated kettles. Nearly three-fourths of the inmates ate in their cells. Breakfast was carried to them in pans on large wooden trays, and dinner was delivered on a slide they passed on the way to their cells.

One of the most valued privileges of the members of the upper-first grade was that of taking their meals in a dining room at tables seating from a dozen to two dozen inmates. The tables were covered with white cloths and furnished with crockery, knives, forks, spoons, and casters. The room was on the first floor of the central building and was connected by a short covered passageway to the kitchen.

In 1891, upper-first-grade men took their meals in the dining room. The meals of lower-first-grade and second-grade men were served to them in their rooms by inmate waiters, designated as "bread-men." According to the rules, when receiving food in their cells, inmates were to take only what they actually needed. Leftover food was to be returned to the bread-man.

In 1891, the breakfast each morning consisted of beef hash, bread, and coffee (made from ground beans and burnt bread) sweetened with sugar. In the evening, bread, molasses, and sugared tea were served. With their last meal of the day, upper-first-grade men had butter and either currant or apple sauce. The bills of fare for dinner were more varied. For instance, mutton stew with potatoes and carrots, vegetable soup, roast beef with gravy, or corned beef with potatoes or cabbage may be served as that day's entrée. Bread was served in liberal quantities, and coffee was allowed to upper-first-grade men daily. The same was served to the lower-first grade four days a week at noon.

In 1891, work in the industrial trades was supplemented by industrial labor, such as in the laundry facility, that could not be classed in the trades schools. Inmates engaged in such work were the office clerks, boiler and dynamo engineers, electric linemen, farmhands, hall men, monitors, bread men, waiters, laundrymen, and teamsters. This work was viewed by management as equally valuable, in terms of reformation, as work in the recognized trades.

On Saturdays, clean clothing was distributed and dirty clothing collected. Each man received with his wash a ticket containing a list of the articles to which he was entitled. Inmates were instructed to observe carefully that they received all they were entitled to and no more. Should there be any surplus or deficiency in their wash, or any article not their own, they were to notify the guard room office through the mail on Monday morning.

In 1892, the daily routine of reformatory life was as follows: at 5:45 a.m., the morning call was sounded for the men to arise and dress; breakfast was served at 6:00 a.m., and half an hour later beds must be made and cells cleaned; at 6:45 a.m., the cell doors were unlocked and the prisoners assembled in squads to carry their buckets to the air galleries and their respective shops; work commenced at 7:00 a.m.; at noon, the whistle sounded for dinner. During the afternoon, on regular days, work was resumed in the shops at 1:00 p.m. and continued until 4:00 p.m.; on Wednesdays and Saturdays, the entire afternoon was devoted to military drill; every secular afternoon at 4:15 p.m., dress parade took place; supper was served at 5:00 p.m. after dress parade; at 7:00 p.m., manual and mental training was provided (these sessions usually lasted until 8:30 p.m., although certain classes sat until 9:00 p.m.); and at 9:30 p.m., taps were sounded and the men retired for the night (those who for important reasons were provided with late light permits were permitted to burn their lights until 11:00 p.m.).

Because of the cost, the ornate original structure had been controversial from the beginning. Nevertheless, the reformatory was built, for the most part, according to architect William Woollett's original design. However, physical changes were made to the facility in the decades after Brockway's departure.

In the late 1930s, the reformatory's pointed turrets were truncated and the Victorian residence that served as the entrance and warden's residence was removed. The gray paint was sandblasted off, and the institution lost its drab and forbidding look.

In this 1930s image, members of the New York Commission of Corrections met at Elmira. The removal of the signature spires on the front facade of the institution can be seen, with scaffolding in the background. The commission strives to provide a safe, stable, and human correctional system and to ensure the delivery of essential services in the correctional setting. To this end, the commission: promulgates minimum standards for the management of correctional facilities; evaluates, investigates, and oversees correctional facilities; assists in developing new correctional facilities; and provides technical assistance.

In the 1940s, artist Ernfred Anderson began work on his sculpture, *Elmira, Builder of Men*.

Two inmates (not pictured) from the Elmira Reformatory posed for Anderson's sculpture.

# *Three*

# The Industrial Trades Program

Wethersfield State Prison in Connecticut is famous primarily for its two outstanding wardens who turned it into a profitable industrial facility. It was at Wethersfield that Brockway became enamored with management's ability to use prison labor for industrial purposes. In 1827, Moses C. Pilsbury was appointed as the first warden at Wethersfield and was succeeded by his son Amos in 1830. In 1845, Amos was appointed superintendent at the Albany County Penitentiary in New York. At age 16, his son Louis Pilsbury started working as a guard in the Albany Penitentiary where his father, Amos, served as superintendent. Upon the death of his father, Amos, Louis D. Pilsbury was appointed superintendent of the Albany prison in 1873. He then accepted the nomination as superintendent of state prisons for New York State in 1879. Amos was one of the five commissioners appointed by Governor Hoffman in 1870 to act as a board of building commissioner for the construction of the reformatory at Elmira. By chapter 207 of the laws of 1876, Louis Pilsbury, the best living exponent of the Auburn prison system, became president of the first board of managers of the New York State Reformatory at Elmira. Zebulon Brockway described his experience at Wethersfield as constituting a "sound and invaluable basis" for management of the Elmira Reformatory, especially with respect to inmate labor. Theoretically, the reformatory was never intended to be self-supporting from the earnings of the inmates; however, Brockway worked hard to make it profitable to the state. By the act of 1876, the board of managers of the reformatory was free to adopt any prison labor system that, in its judgment, was most conducive to reformation. The board opted for the public account system, wherein the employment of the convicts was in all respects directed by the state, and the products of their labor were sold on the open market for the benefit of the state. The reformatory was considered among the pioneers in trades training, having adopted it early because of its peculiar fitness and advantage to the prisoners.

Early in 1878, a small force of inmates began the manufacture of brushes. In this illustration and in the photograph below, some remarkably young inmates are at work making brushes.

In 1881, a legislative committee found that the management of the reformatory had entered into a league with two other prisons outside of the state for the purpose of controlling the market in brushes. Consequently, the State of New York banned further production on the so-called state account system and installed the contract system of prison labor.

By 1879, the population of prisoners had reached 485; about two-thirds of the available men were employed in the manufacture of brushes. Hollowware production was in the beginning stages, thus little money had been made from it at that point. It was believed by Superintendent Brockway that the reformatory could be self-supporting from its manufacturing operations. Brush-making was the chief industry in 1879 and had generated revenue over the year. While the productive industries at Elmira had been eliminated by law in 1888, the various industrial classes in the new trades school building were introduced in January 1886. Systematic trade training was conducted in three connected, Greek cross–shaped, one-story pavilions in the eastern yard that afforded 27,000 square feet of floor room. In 1890, the nearly 40 trades and industries taught (such as chair-making, pictured above) increased the percentage of reformations to more than 80 percent.

By 1890, there was a cooking school with six ranges for instruction. Stained-glass windows for the enlarged lecture hall were being made by two prisoners. A large number of industries were taught, and care was taken to assign the prisoners to work for which they were best fitted. The great variety of industries taught in the institution in 1890 included, class 1—trade classes for production and instruction, such as iron molding, brass molding, bookbinding, baking, printing and typesetting, tailoring, shoe-making, upholstering, cabinetmaking, finishing and varnishing, and boat-building; class 2—trade classes for instruction only, such as machinery, blacksmithing, stone-cutting, plastering, pattern-making, frescoing, carpentry, wood-turning, woodcarving, hardwood finishing, plumbing, bricklaying, stenography, brass finishing, tin-smithing, barbering, and music; and class 3—state mechanical roles, such as engineers, plumbers, painters, carpenters, bricklayers, tending bricklayers stonemasons, tending stonemasons, and laborers on prison grounds. A band from the class 2 music instruction is pictured here.

Instruction and production in 1891 included the hardware department; cabinet-making department; boat department; novelty department; packing case department; umbrella department; tinware; broom-making; and electrical and marine supply.

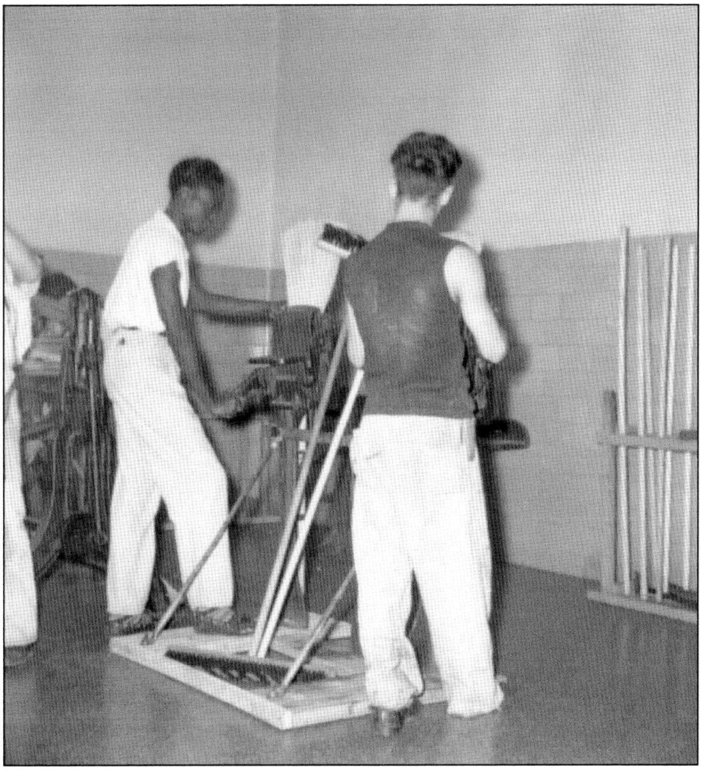

A wage-earning system was established on October 1, 1891, to give each prisoner an earning capacity that allowed him to subsist by his own efforts while incarcerated. Pictured is an inmate making a broom.

In 1891, student work began in the carpentry class with the use of the ripper and the coarse- and fine-crosscut saws. Among other things, students were taught to file their own saws and keep them in good order. The carpentry work of the institution was done by the members of this class under the supervision of an experienced citizen instructor. Students in the cabinet-making class were given considerable practice on "dummy" work and, eventually, were working on side boards, joining the parts as they came from the machine room and fitting the locks, trimmings, and plate glass. Major items produced in this department in 1891 were tables, chairs, lounges, sofas, and ottomans. The production of these items afforded an opportunity for the approximately 40 students to put into application what they had learned.

In 1891, the bookbindery was located close to the printing office and was an important adjunct to it. The instructor was an experienced man, and the course of study and practice was very comprehensive and complete.

The final examination in this department consisted of binding an entire book.

In 1891, the foundry was a portion of the hardware-manufacturing plant, and the trade class pupils in it began to shape articles for the market when they had been taught the first principles of iron molding. Beside the foundry and its cupola was a hardware plant with all the necessary machinery, tools, and appliances for transforming a piece of pig iron into a finely finished merchantable piece of shelf hardware.

There were 120 inmates employed in the department, with 50 in the foundry and 70 in the finishing shop and packing room.

The machinist class was another popular course among the inmates. In 1891, there were accommodations for 50 men in the two sections of the class.

The machinist class began with 25 lessons on the chipping of small blocks. The pupils took up drilling and biting holes in flat iron, round iron, and biting boxes.

The final examination of the members of the machinist class consisted of general repair work, thereby fully demonstrating the student's ability to handle tools and material to "his own and employers' advantage outside." By 1890, there had been in operation a thoroughly equipped tinsmith class. Initially established for production purposes only, the tin shop was eventually carried on solely for instructional purposes. Moreover, it was maintained for the general repairs necessary in an institution such as the reformatory.

To learn the art of horseshoeing, an experimental class was established in 1890 from the students in the blacksmithing shop.

According to the *1891 Annual Report of the Board of Managers*, very little difficulty was encountered by the graduates from the blacksmith and horseshoeing shops in finding work on the outside. It was one of the most useful trades school classes.

Barbering was classed among the domestic features, although it was one of the most useful of the trades school classes. In 1891, it was located in the No. 1 trade school building (see the 1891 floor plan), where about 20 members of the so-called barbering class manned a dozen chairs.

Pictured below, inmates receive haircuts in a cell block, perhaps in the disciplinary unit.

In 1891, the tailoring class had about 50 members. All the wearing apparel used in the institution was manufactured in the tailor shop. Blue suits were made for the upper-first-grade men, black and grey for those in the first or neutral grade, and red suits for the third grade. Repairs were kept up on all articles, and clothes were furnished of a pattern suitable for the man released on parole.

In 1888, articles commonly needed and used at the reformatory, such as clothing and other necessary supplies, were already being made by the inmates.

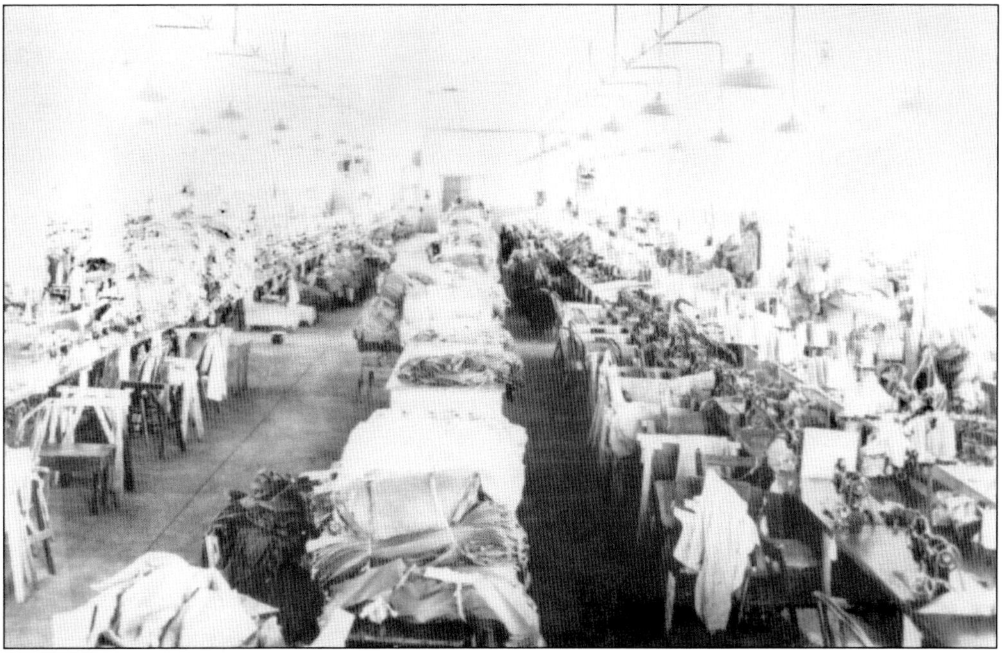

In 1892, three new industries were added, and the manufacture of clothing was one of them. In 1893, a clothing-cutting class was added to the trades school. It afforded instruction principally to members of the tailoring class. The latter was a day class, and the clothing cutting was an evening class. Sessions met twice a week.

Prior to 1888, shoe-making was one of the productive industries. By 1891, it was confined generally to the manufacture and mending of boots and shoes for inmates. Novices in this work were set at the making of waxed ends, blind stitching, square and hollow stitching, lasting, stocking, pegging and nailing, and heeling and trimming. Next was bottom finishing and treeing. The course also afforded general instruction in different kinds of leather and the cutting-out of work.

The final test, before men graduated from the class, consisted in the making, without aid, of a pair of boots or shoes. This class was not organized upon the principle of the division of labor but after the plan of the village shoe shop. The greater part of the experience obtained was in connection with the more common shoes of the majority of inmates.

There was, however, a good deal of work done on a finer grade of shoe (those worn by the upper-first-grade men).

Additionally, practice in the handling of still finer shoes came in the repairing of the boots and shoes of citizens employed as officers and staff at the reformatory.

In 1891, the curriculum, as arranged in the stenography and typewriting class, anticipated the graduation of shorthand writers capable of taking dictation of ordinary business at the rate of at least 120 words a minute within a year.

All pupils learning trades in which the knowledge of drafting was necessary or helpful had a place in the mechanical drawing class, which had on its rolls 300 to 400 names at a time.

In 1891, the mechanical drawing class was divided into three sections, and each of these sections was divided into 11 graded subdivisions containing 6 to 20 students.

In 1891, the equipment of the fresco painting classroom, in which this trade was taught, accommodated 30 people. When the pupil developed sufficient facility, he was given work on the walls and ceilings wherever decoration was required. In 1892, the pupils in the new sign-painting class were selected upon the basis of some special aptitude or taste for the work. Graduates were capable of earning, when released, wages of $2 per day. In this photograph, students are painting the ceiling and upper part of the shop as part of the fresco painting class.

Instruction in 34 different trades was imparted in 1893. The total attendance in the trades school numbered 1,804 inmates in 1893. Pictured here is a trades school building.

In addition to the trades already mentioned, courses included boat-building, brass finishing, brass molding, hardwood finishing, pattern-making, photography and etching, plumbing, printing, upholstery, wood-carving, wood-turning, and mechanical woodworking. Shown here are smoke billows from the industrial shops located in the western yard of the institution.

# *Four*

# The Educational Program

Between 1867 and 1877, the Elmira Reformatory developed into the institution it was intended to be; that is, a moral hospital for young felons in need of an education or trade training. For the founders and managers of the reformatory, the problem with the delinquent or criminal was at its foundation an educational one. Thus, the teaching of practical morality and trade training in such a way as to form good habits of living was the surest preventative of a criminal career. Practically speaking, intellectual and vocational reform meant moral reform at Elmira. Indeed, the reformatory was established because crime was equated with immorality. For at least 20 years (1867–1887), this idea was the guiding principle and was at the core of the system of prison discipline developed at the Elmira Reformatory. The managers pointed out that at least 40 percent of the young men committed to Elmira were ignorant in the most primary branches of an English education. The Elmira system contemplated a penitentiary of compulsory education. It differed from other institutions not in its educational theories, but in its feature of compulsion. The individuals with whom it had to deal rendered such compulsion necessary. Intellectual development was to be accomplished in the schoolroom by studies and lessons according to the capacity of the pupil. The disciplinary use of this was to "invigorate the mind and strengthen the will-power," thus driving "low and sordid ideas" out from the mind, replacing them with others of a totally different kind. The prison school was organized on March 16, 1877, and all the prisoners, unless incapacitated, were required to attend. The number of students at that time was 170. There were 20 teachers (of which 17 were prisoners qualified by their examination and instruction) in the normal department, which met on Wednesday evenings. Initially, prisoners attended only for recitations on Tuesday and Friday evenings for 90 minutes.

By 1900, all of the prisoners' time was fully occupied (without producing any goods of marketable value) with trades school activities designed to fit them for free life.

While the various industrial classes in the new trades school building were introduced in January 1886, the educational program was established in 1878. Initially, classes were arranged in the evening so as not to interfere with the hours of labor and included all the men who were able to attend. The three-times-a-week recitations, which were attended by all inmates, were divided into six large classes overseen by experienced teachers. The whole educational program, under the supervision of the Reverend Dr. D.R. Ford of Elmira College, covered two years.

The final organization of the school of letters was completed in October 1879. All 500 men were studying math, 400 were regularly drilled in reading and spelling, 100 were studying geography, 98 were drilled in single-entry bookkeeping suitable for farmers and mechanics, 100 men of the highest class studied the principles of civil government, and 100 covered a course in American history. There were special classes in German, Italian, and French for the benefit of those desiring a better acquaintance with English. In 1879, of the 246 indefinites, 151 of them (61 percent) were foreign-born: Irish (83) 33.7 percent; German (41) 16.6 percent; English (9) 3.6 percent; Hebrew (6) 2.4 percent; French (5) 2.0 percent; African (4) 1.6 percent; Scottish (2) 0.8 percent; and Italian (1) 0.4 percent. Ninety-five of them (38.6 percent) were American-born.

On July 22, 1883, the first lecture of a course on practical morality was delivered by Charles A. Collin, Esq., of the Elmira bar, to the higher-level classes. Another historic event occurred on Thursday (Thanksgiving Day), November 29, 1883 when the first issue of the *Summary* was published. The first prison newspaper in American history, the *Summary* began as an eight-page weekly digest of world and local news. In every detail, it was the product of inmate talent (engravers, printers, and pressmen).

By 1888, all inmates were required to attend the school of letters, the sessions of which were held every evening Monday through Friday. The teachers were among some of the very best to be found in the city of Elmira and areas nearby. The lecture method of teaching was uniformly followed by all instructors. No school books were issued to the students; rather, each lesson was printed on a leaflet and distributed to the pupils, one lesson at a time. All students were subjected to monthly written examinations, the results of which would either favorably or unfavorably affect their progress toward release. There were classes in political economy, civil government, practical ethics, English literature, language, physics, arithmetic, and algebra.

By 1893, the school of letters was coordinated with the military and trades school and was the center of educational work. It included the following: a kindergarten and normal class for student teachers; instruction classes in elementary branches; lecture divisions in history, ethics, literature, and natural science; a library; two weekly newspapers; courses of lectures; and musical and artistic entertainments. The secretary classified the new inmates for participation in the school of letters according to their relative abilities.

The staff of the school of letters during 1897 consisted of a resident school director, a non-resident lecturer in literature, history, ethics and nature studies, and a normal class of inmate teachers (from 30 to 40 in number) under the training and direction of the school director. The school director also had an inmate secretary, much like the one pictured above, who carried on the clerical work connected with the school of letters.

In 1897, there was a language class for foreigners who came to the reformatory entirely ignorant of the English language. They were taught as many useful and common words and phrases as possible. Nothing but English was allowed to be spoken in the class. The instructors had been selected—in a manner that had, since 1878, become the usual—from among the inmates themselves. These men constituted the normal class, pictured here, and were chosen after a careful consideration of their education and ability. The normal class met with the school director (for an hour twice each week) for training and instruction in the work of teaching. Before he was given a class to teach, each man was required to visit a class and make a report on what he observed.

By 1900, grading was done by the school director. After a personal interview and examination of each man, he was assigned to one of the three grades of the school.

There were three large divisions in the school of letters arranged for lecture purposes. The ethics division consisted of 300 men that met on Tuesday evenings to study history and on Friday evenings to discuss ethical principles. The second large division consisted of 450 men who met on Sunday mornings for instruction in some line of nature study. The third large division of 450 men was the most illiterate in the institution. They met every Sunday for elementary instruction in American history and biography.

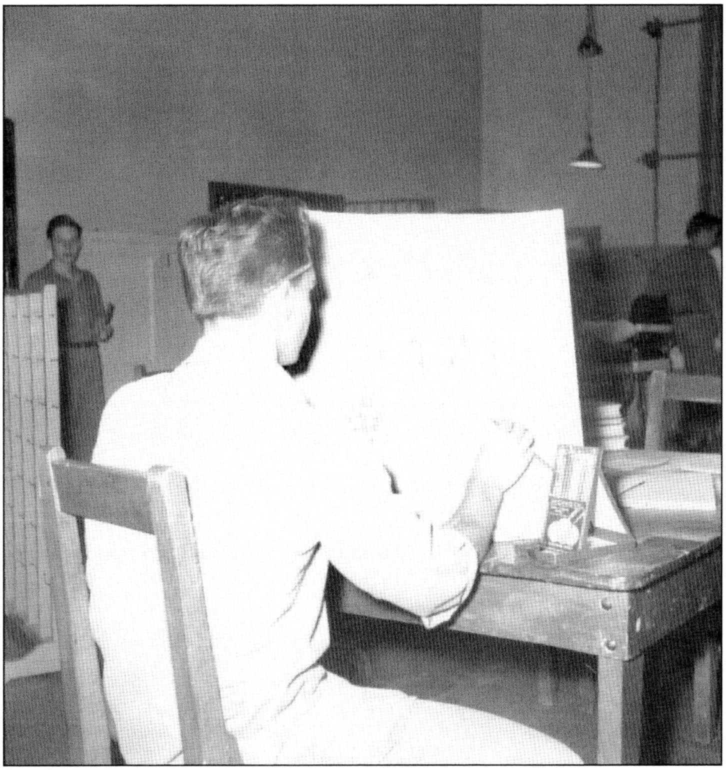

There was a lower class of extreme defectives, for which kindergarten instruction was required. The foreigners unable to speak or write English were placed in a class by themselves, and as rapidly as possible were taught the elements of English.

By 1889, track-and-field events were conducted at Elmira. The reformatory was the first correctional institution to use games such as baseball, basketball, football, and track-and-field as "treatment" rather than mere diversion. Such activities were duly noted regularly in the *Summary*. The reformatory contained a community differing from others not more in its compulsory isolation than in the homogeneous character of its life. The conditions and requirements of its aims and methods were not left to voluntary choice.

The reformatory baseball team is pictured playing the Willys-Knight team, which is pictured out on the field. The reformatory horse and cow barn can be seen behind the grandstand.

Pictured is another view of the baseball field. Athletic events were more than just recreation; they were an important part of the Elmira Reformatory's system of prison discipline

The amount of sleep, the diet, amount and modes of bodily exercise, and labor and amusements were all an intelligent provision for the common good of the whole body. Pictured is the reformatory's basketball team.

Although sporting events such as baseball were important, the unique feature of life at Elmira was its educational program, especially in the form of classroom school work. All inmates were part of the educational department, as students, teachers, or clerical assistants. The educational program was at the heart of the Elmira system of prison discipline.

# *Five*

# The Physical Culture Program

For five months in 1886, as indicted in the board of managers' annual report, an experiment of physical treatment for mental and moral improvement had been in progress at the reformatory. A group of 12 inmates of the "lowest type," who were "apparently incorrigible," were specially selected for the experiment. The group consisted of 10 white and 2 black prisoners. There were no indications of disease of the nervous, respiratory, vascular, or digestive systems. Five men had skin disorders that were commonly seen in penal institutions and "provoked or aggravated by well-known causes." The average age was 23, with 19 and 29 representing the extremes. Under the direction of Dr. Hamilton Wey, they were subjected to a special diet, baths with massages, systematic physical exercise, and special "mental drills." The reason for the formation of the class was to determine whether physical culture in the form of frequent baths, massages, and daily calisthenics (under the care of a competent instructor) could result in a "partial awakening and stimulation of dormant mental power." The experiment was reasonably successful according to Brockway, who wrote enthusiastically that: "With suitable baths and exercising hall I would apply the treatment to fully 150 of our men here, feeling confident many would thereby be saved whose conduct, after release, is otherwise un-assured. It is very important that a considerable number of the inmates should have a thorough and thoroughly scientific course of physical treatment, for the mental quickening to be accomplished by this means." Between 1889 and 1893, the close relationship between corporeal (of the body) conditions and mental operations was completely accepted as the most advanced system of prison discipline. Physical education as a means of reformation became an indispensable procedure for approximately 10 percent of the criminals at Elmira. For Brockway, at least by 1889, reformation was a purely scientific process. The physical improvement of the prisoners was, however, only part of the end in view. With the quickening of the physical forces came a marked alertness of the mental faculties.

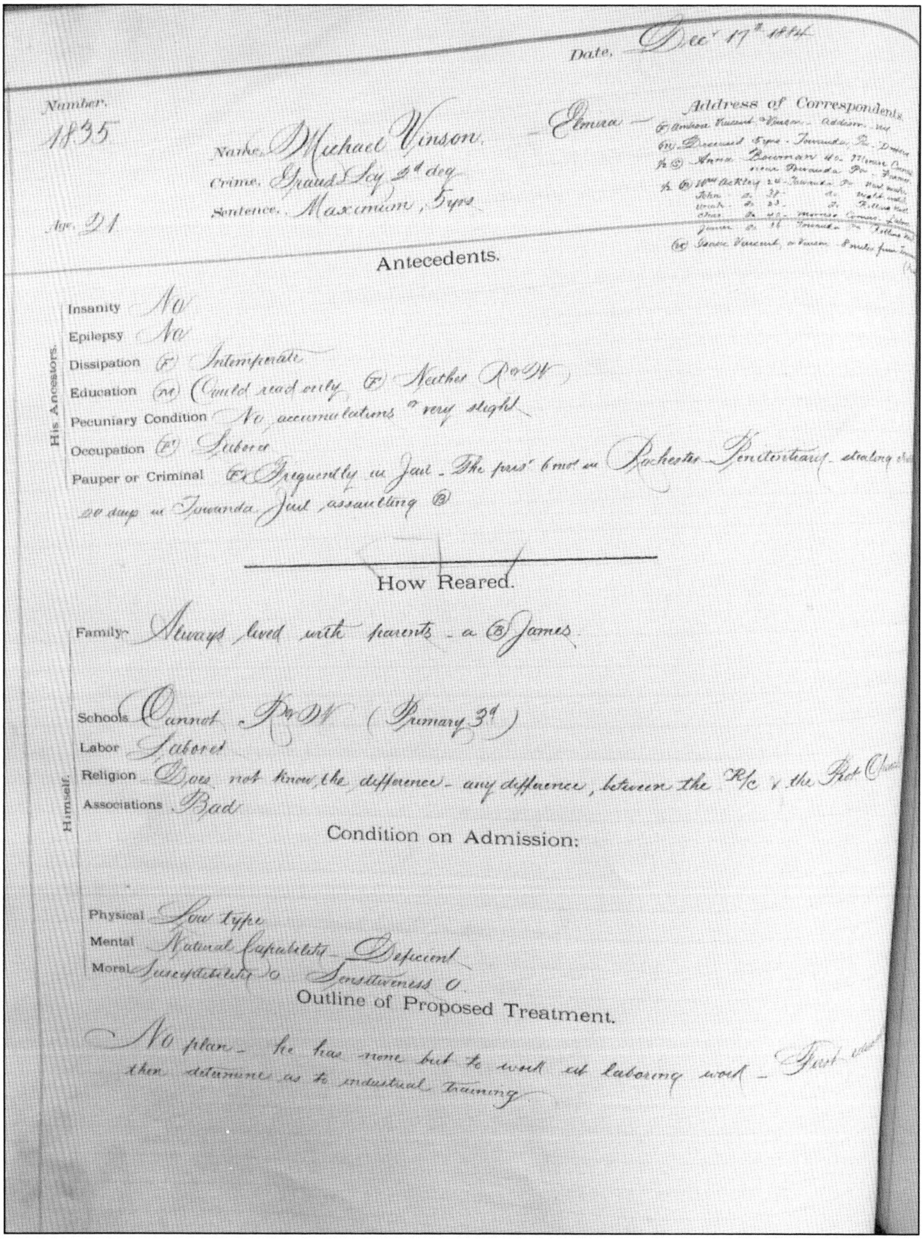

Date, Dec 17th 1884

Number. 1835

Name, Michael Vinson. — Elmira —

Crime, Grand Lcy 2d deg

Sentence, Maximum, 5yrs

Age, 21

Address of Correspondents

Antecedents.

His Ancestors.

Insanity No

Epilepsy No

Dissipation (F) Intemperate

Education (M) Could read only (F) Neither R & W

Pecuniary Condition No accumulations very slight

Occupation (F) Laborer

Pauper or Criminal (F) Frequently in Jail - The past 6 mos in Rochester Penitentiary, stealing

20 days in Towanda Jail, assaulting (B)

How Reared.

Family— Always lived with parents - a (B) James

Himself.

Schools Cannot R & W (Primary 3d)

Labor Laborer

Religion Does not know the difference - any difference, between the R/C & the Prot Ch

Associations Bad

Condition on Admission:

Physical Low type

Mental Natural Capabilities — Deficient

Moral Susceptibility 0 Sensitiveness 0

Outline of Proposed Treatment.

No plan - he has none but to work at laboring work - First

then determine as to industrial training

One of the subjects of the experiment was Michael Vinson. All of his personal information is contained in the biographical register, pictured here. Each new inmate met with Superintendent Brockway for an examination of his entire life history. From the biographical register, it is known that inmate Michael Vinson (No. 1835) was 23 years old when admitted for second-degree grand larceny on December 17, 1884. According to Superintendent Brockway's handwritten entry, Vinson had no history of insanity or epilepsy in his family. His father—an intemperate, illiterate, impoverished laborer—was frequently in jail for stealing chickens. Inmate Vinson's mother was deceased; he had always lived with his parents and one sibling. He could not read or write and did not know the difference between the Roman Catholic church and the Protestant church. Brockway reported that all of Vinson's associations or peers were simply "bad."

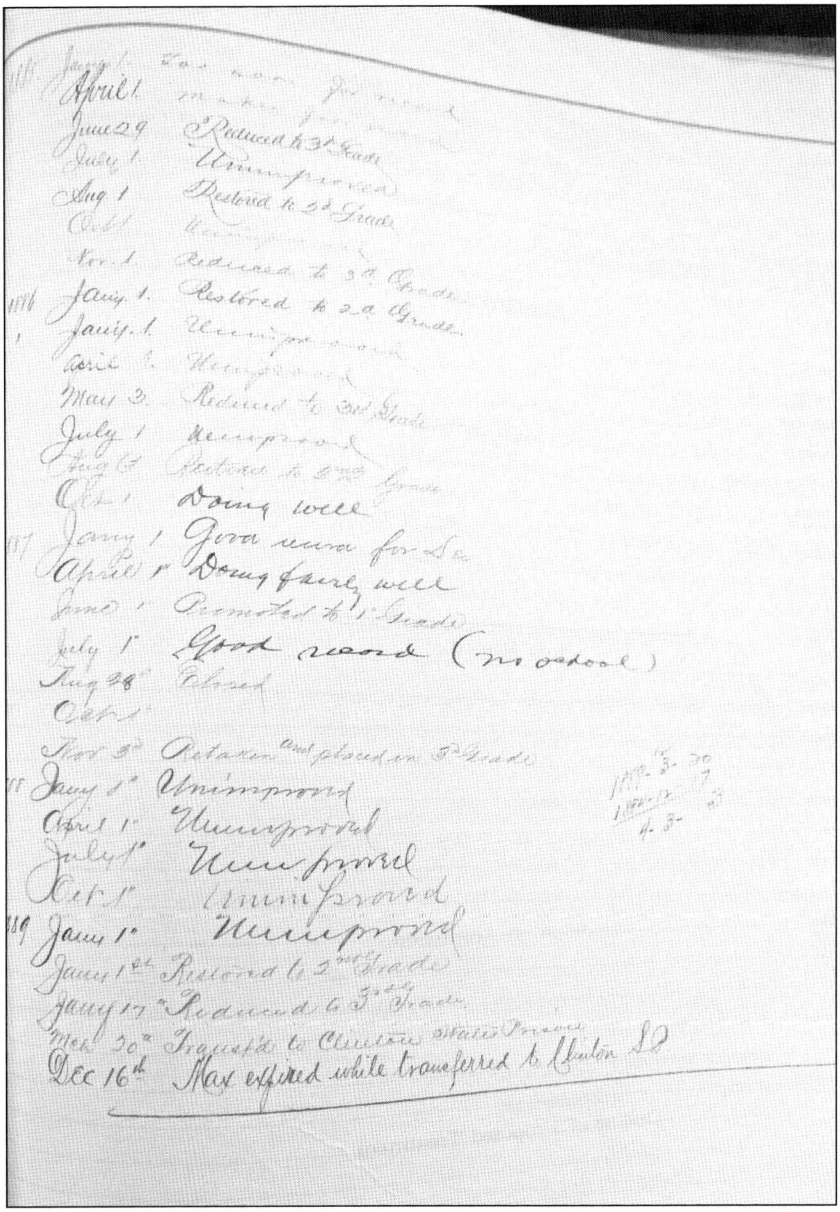

April 1
June 29 Reduced to 3rd Grade
July 1 Unimproved
Aug 1 Restored to 2d Grade
Nov. 1 Reduced to 3d Grade
1886 Jany. 1. Restored to 2d Grade
Jany. 1. Unimproved
May 3. Reduced to 3rd Grade
July 1 Unimproved
Oct 1 Doing well
1887 Jany 1 Good ... for ...
April 1 Doing fairly well
June 1 Promoted to 1st Grade
July 1 Good record (no school)
Aug 28 Eloped
Nov 3rd Retaken and placed in 3rd Grade
1888 Jany 1st Unimproved
April 1st Unimproved
July 1st Unimproved
Oct 1st Unimproved
1889 Jany 1st Unimproved
Jany 1st Restored to 2nd Grade
Jany 17 Reduced to 3rd Grade
Mch 20th Transf'd to Clinton State Prison
Dec 16th Max expired while transferred to Clinton SP

Superintendent Brockway also recorded that inmate Michael Vinson's physical condition at the time of admission was of the "low type." Furthermore, his mental "natural capability" was "deficient," and he had zero "moral susceptibility" and zero "sensitiveness" to moral persuasion. The register also notes that Vinson did not do well at the reformatory. In fact, he served all five years of his five-year sentence. The average stay for an inmate at the reformatory on a five-year sentence was only 14 months. After having been received at the reformatory on December 17, 1884, and placed in the second grade (as all inmates were classified upon arrival), Vinson's progress was documented as follows: "June 29, 1885: reduced to third grade; Jan. 1, 1886: restored to second grade; June 1, 1887: promoted to first grade; Aug. 28, 1887: escaped; Jan. 1, 1889: restored to second grade; March 20, 1889: transferred to Clinton State Prison; Dec. 16, 1889: Max expired while transferred to Clinton State Prison."

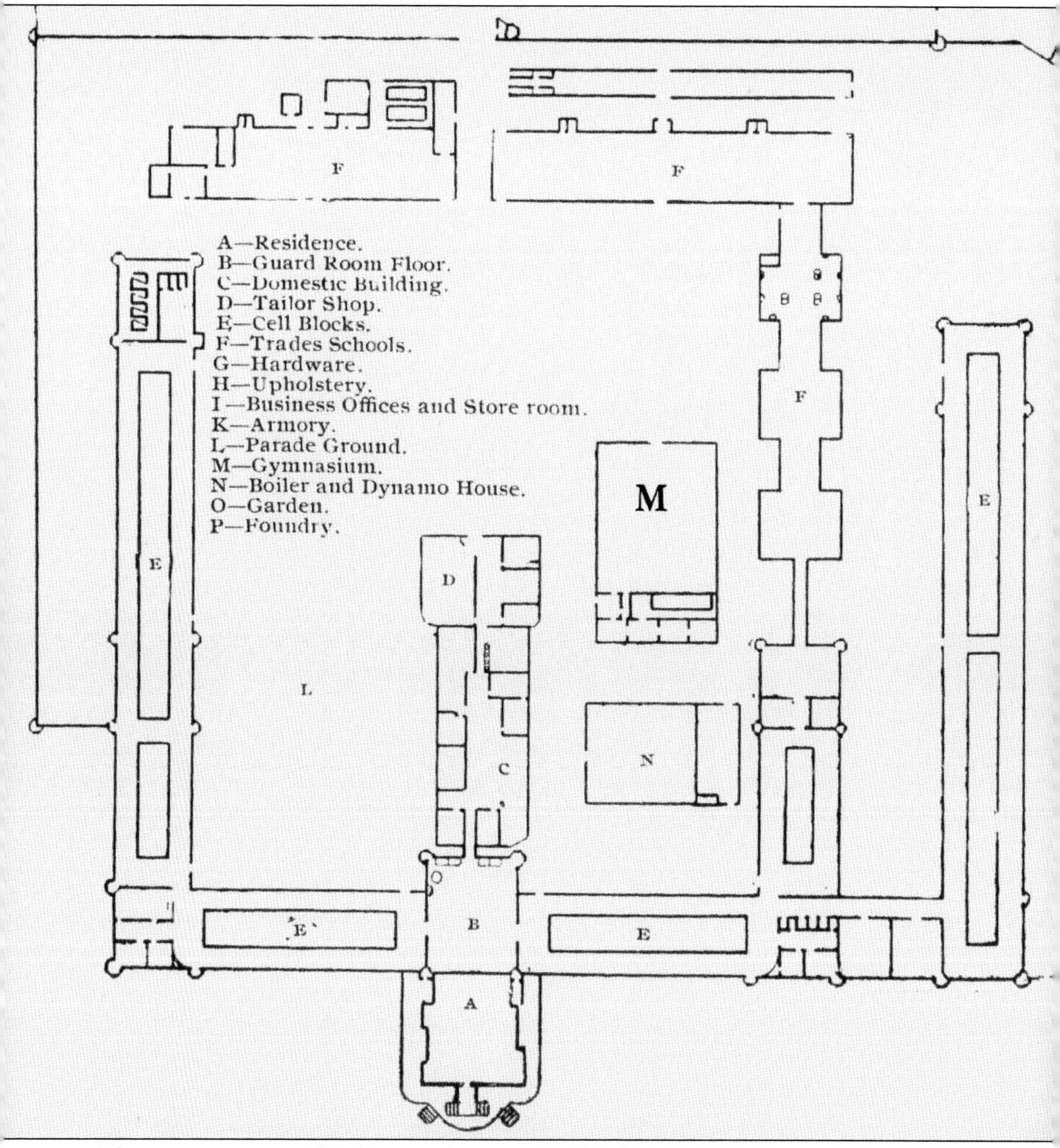


The gymnasium, completed in March 1890, was a brick structure 140 feet in length by 80 feet in width. It stood near the center of the original reformatory enclosure. It contained a large exercising hall (100 feet long by 80 feet wide) and bathrooms (60 feet long by 40 feet wide), which included two showers. There was also a drying room and a plunge room with a swimming pool (with spring board attached) 12 feet wide by 47 feet long and 6 feet deep. The building was heated by steam and lighted and ventilated by 50 large windows. Extending around the four sides of the gymnasium proper, about 10 feet from the floor, was a padded gallery for running that was one-sixteenth of a mile in length.

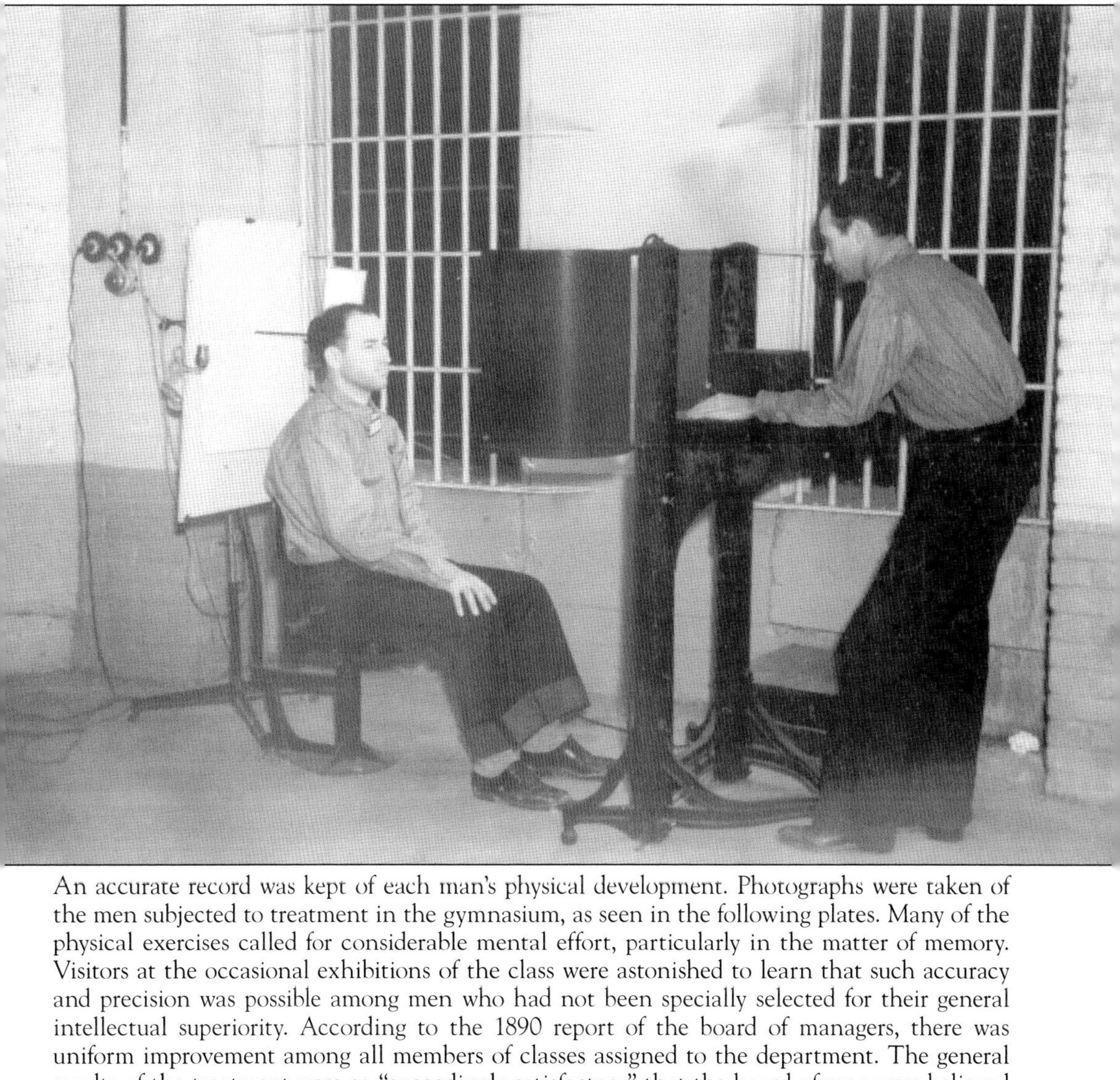

An accurate record was kept of each man's physical development. Photographs were taken of the men subjected to treatment in the gymnasium, as seen in the following plates. Many of the physical exercises called for considerable mental effort, particularly in the matter of memory. Visitors at the occasional exhibitions of the class were astonished to learn that such accuracy and precision was possible among men who had not been specially selected for their general intellectual superiority. According to the 1890 report of the board of managers, there was uniform improvement among all members of classes assigned to the department. The general results of the treatment were so "exceedingly satisfactory" that the board of managers believed it would retain its important position among the reformative influences of the reformatory. The following plates were created by Dr. Wey in 1892.

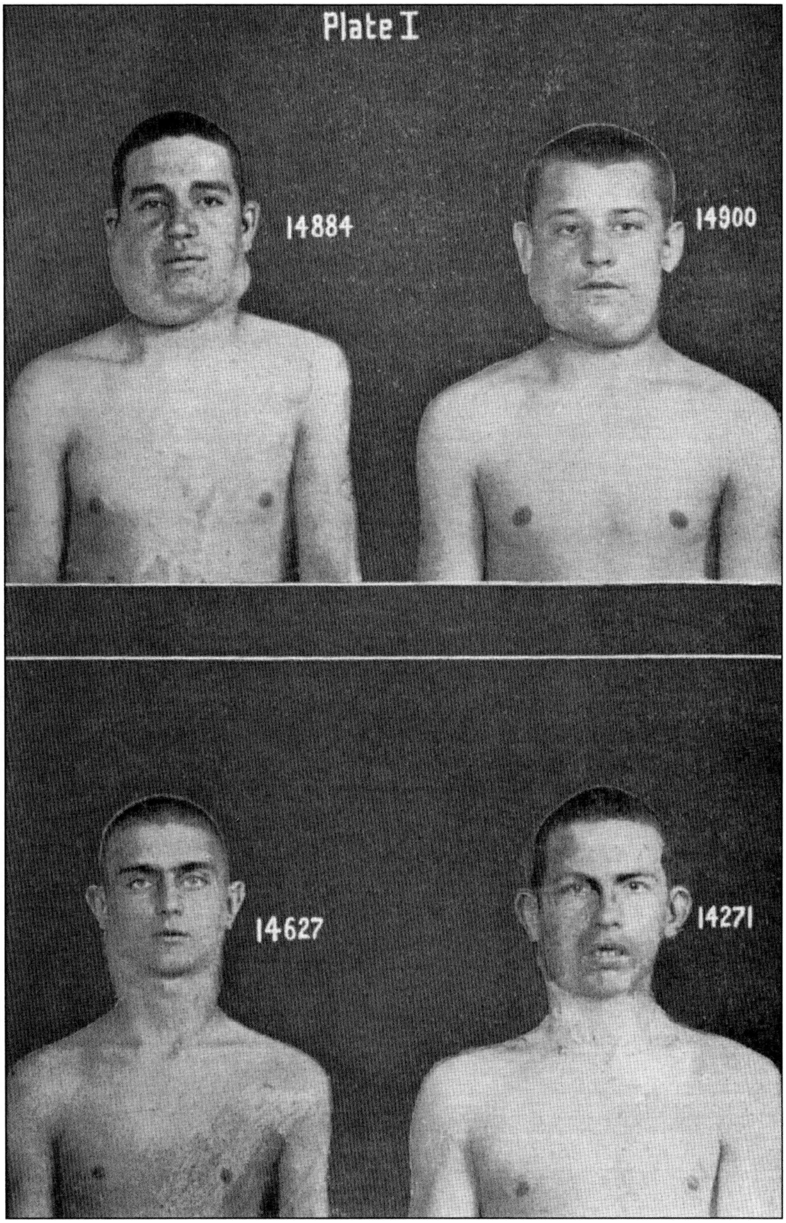


Nos. 14884 and 14900 showed enlargement of the salivary glands situated on each side behind the lower jaw. In the case of No. 14627, the glands of the neck were implicated (the swelling of the right side being behind one of two thick muscles that move the head from side to side). In No. 14271, the glands are situated above the collarbone. In three of the cases pictured, the inflammation of the lymph nodes was a consequence of influenza. Cases of this variety were unfitted for shop work, which aggravated the trouble, and, as the hospital afforded insufficient facilities for exercise, the best disposal was assignment to the gymnasium. The improved hygienic conditions and the effect upon vegetative functions—digestion, assimilation, circulation, secretion, and excretion—resulting from exercise and bathing, supplemented by an extra diet, placed these unfortunates in the best position to combat a disease from which recovery was discouragingly delayed.

Both the warm and hot rooms were furnished with hardwood settees arranged in tiers of three, one above the other, upon which the men sat during the sweating process. Designed especially for the physical culture department were a series of baths that were "equal in their general utility to those in the best athletic clubs in the country." These privileges were highly appreciated by those in the class and by many other prisoners in the reformatory; however, they belonged solely to those in the physical culture class. The same restriction was applicable to the extensive paraphernalia in the gymnasium (pictured here). In the baths, massage treatment was resorted to under the personal supervision of the instructor, and the general treatment was often regulated according to the demands of special cases. In the apparatus work, particular attention was always paid to individual physical defects, and each man got the full benefit of all general training.

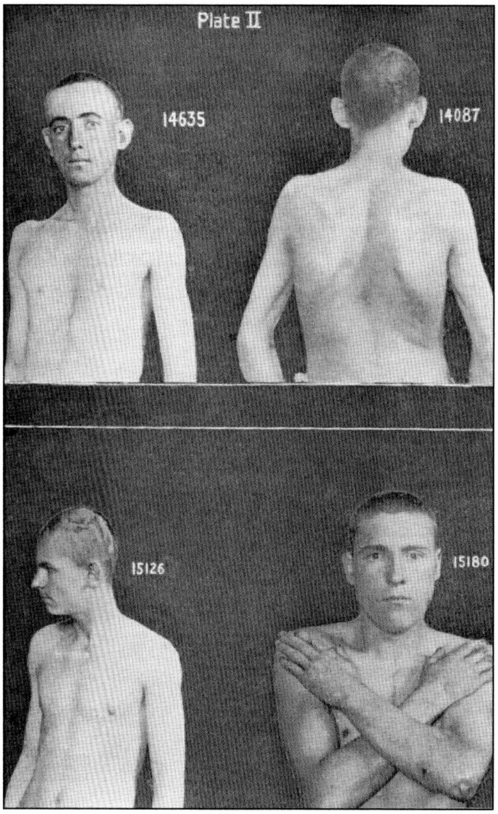


According to Dr. Wey, No. 14635 in plate II was a case where the curvature of the breastbone formed a depression of sufficient size to admit a finger one-inch deep. The companion picture on the plate, No. 14087, presented curvature of the spinal column. No. 15126 showed traces of ringworm of the scalp, and No. 15180 had inflamed patches of skin upon both hands, his left forearm, and elbow.

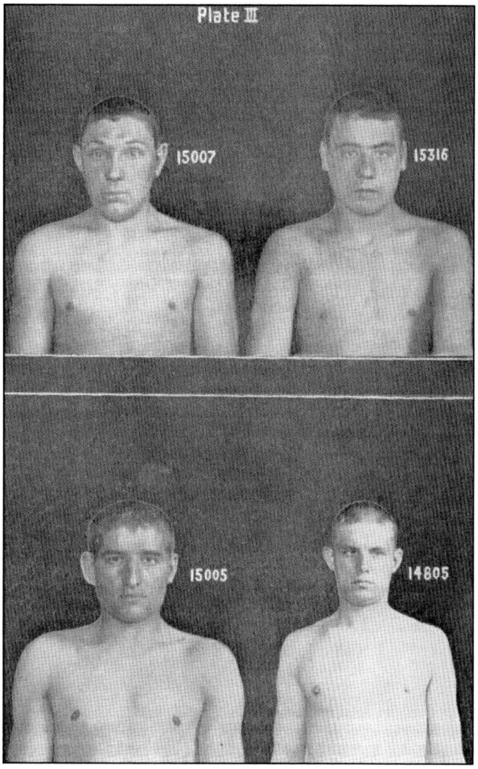


This class, of which four illustrations appear in plate III, was deficient in nervous energy, easily taking on flesh like a stall-fed ox. With this class, physical education promoted habits of obedience, mental concentration, and application, and forced into the background the former man. The men portrayed here were illiterate at the time of admission, devoid of affection for place or person, and with moral natures undeveloped.

Instances of sexual perversion and exaggeration are shown in plate IV. The gymnasium afforded a means of treatment for this class of offenders. The expenditure of nervous energy in exercise and training, the stimulating influences of healthy competition, bathing, and the induction of fatigue within physiological limits tended to diminish erotic desires and produced a better man.

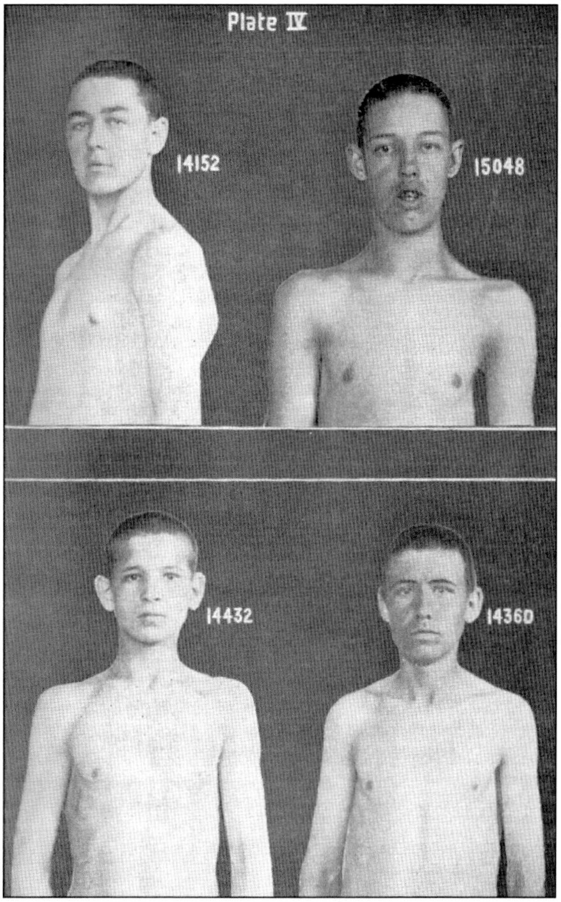


Once insane, No. 13243 was inclined to obesity and was as heavy mentally as physically.

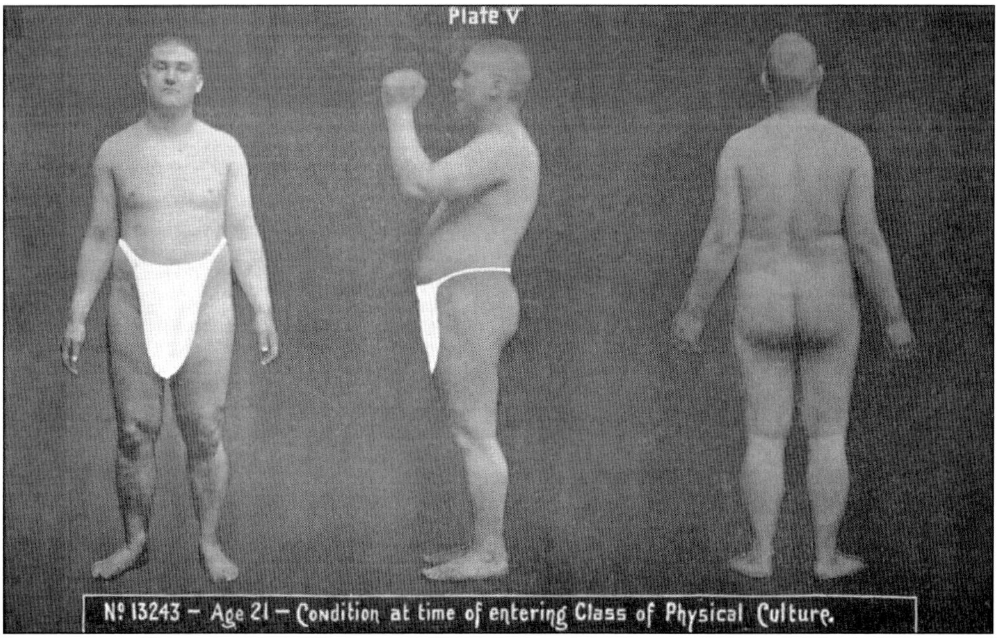

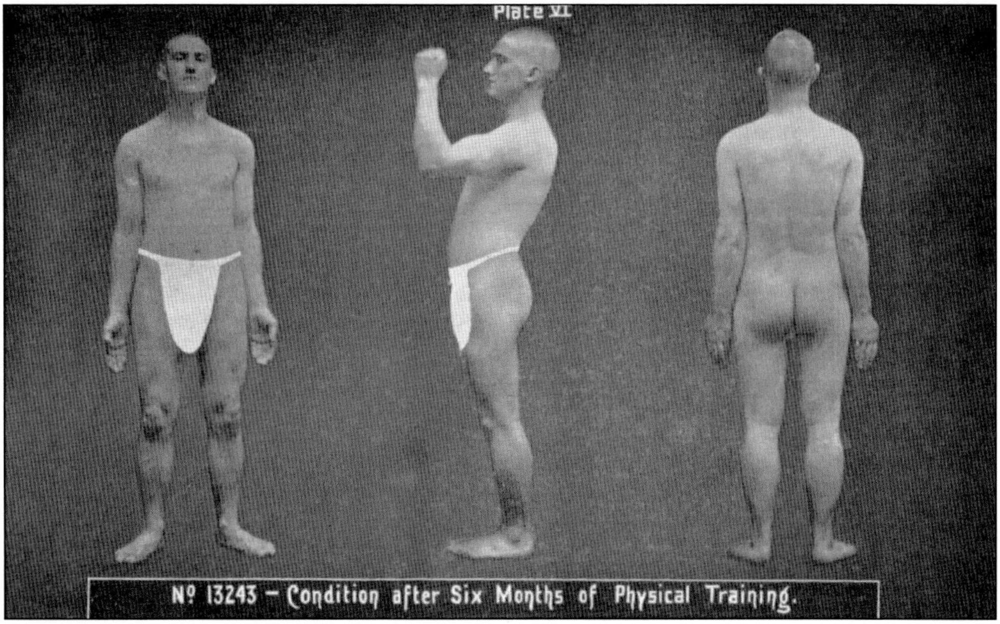


The improvement was shown in the reduction of adipose tissue and the increased muscular power conferred. Organic life was quickened and inertia of voluntary parts overcome. He was eventually discharged upon parole.

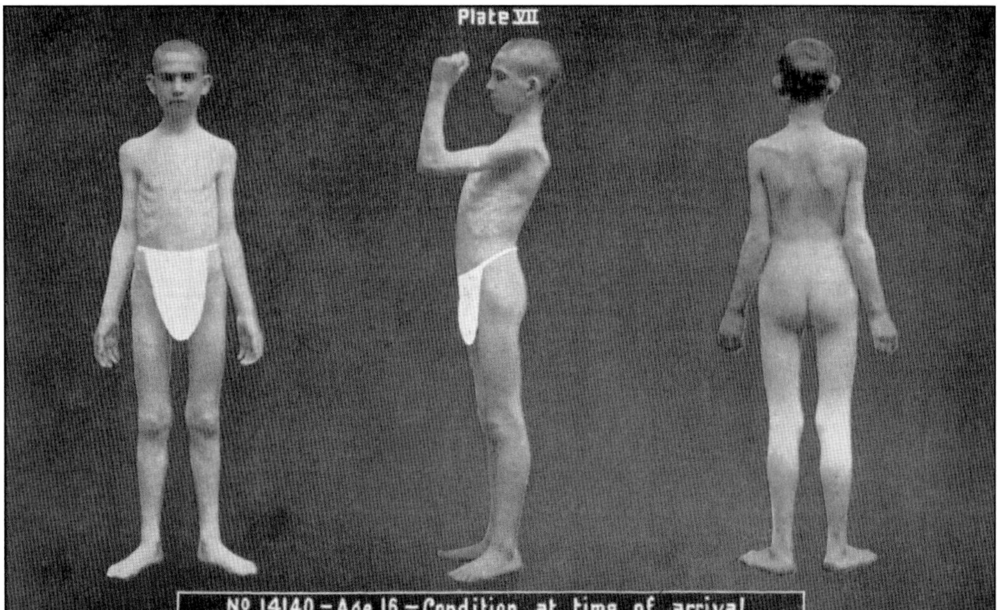


No. 14140 was anemic with feeble circulation and shortness of breath and was in a state of general deterioration.

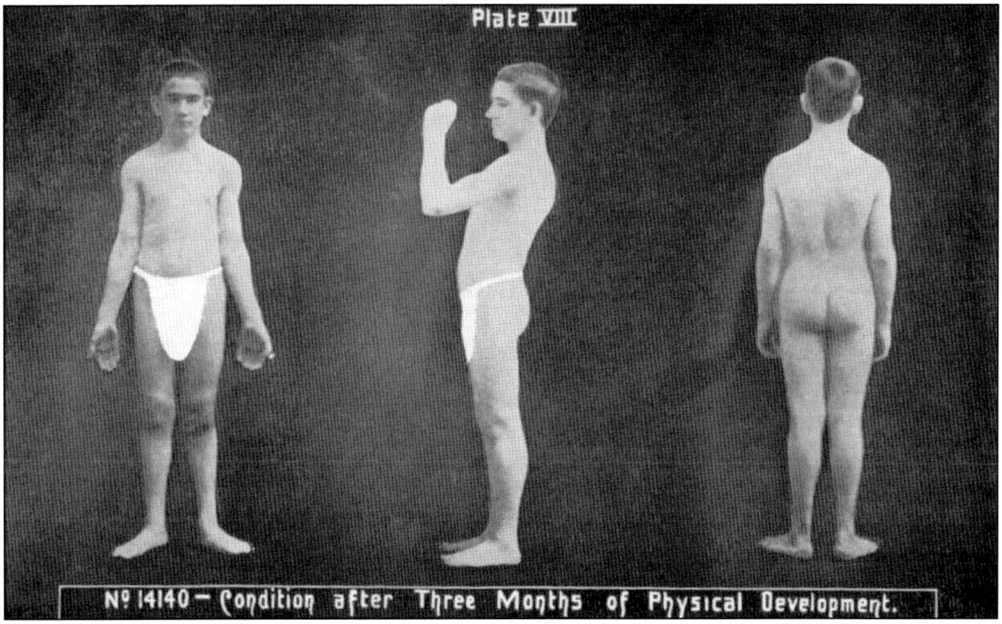


Systematized work with the stimulation of baths and rubbing increased No. 14140's weight by 13 pounds in three months. At the time of his discharge, he was in good health and was a proficient wood turner. This was another case in which the gymnasium was a substitute for the hospital.

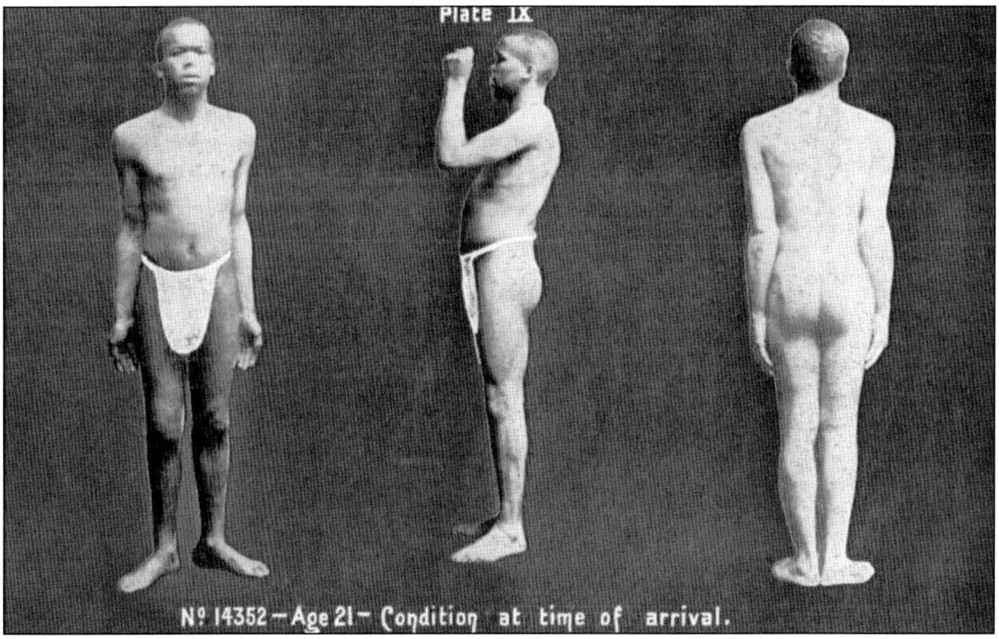


No. 14352 was selected to overcome a swollen and stiff knee resulting from a puncture wound and subsequent abscess. He was fairly nourished but crippled from the inability to use the knee.

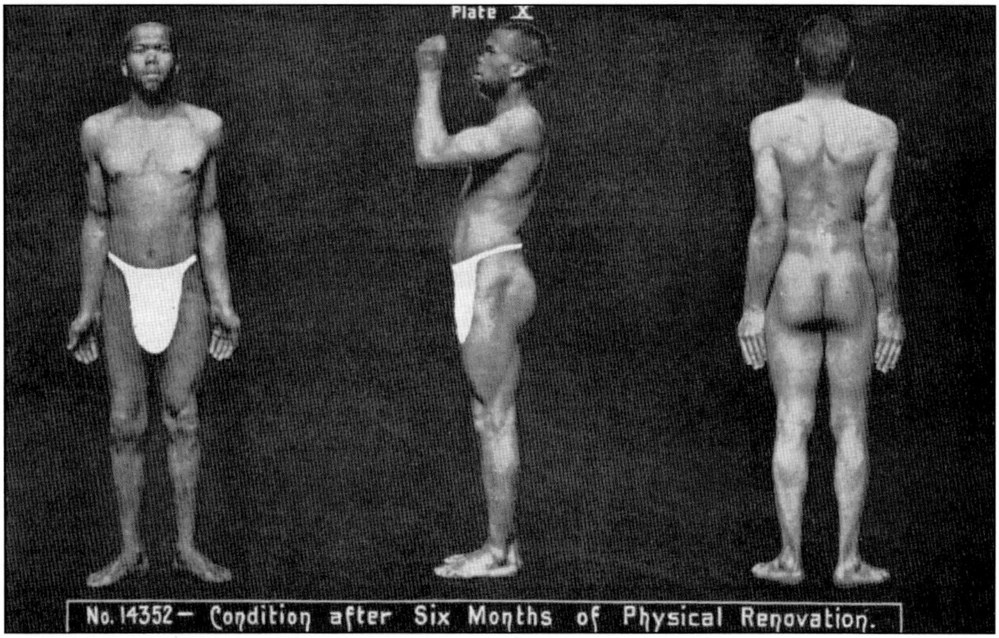


The original appearance of the swollen joint is well shown in plate IX on the previous page; this plate presents a striking contrast.

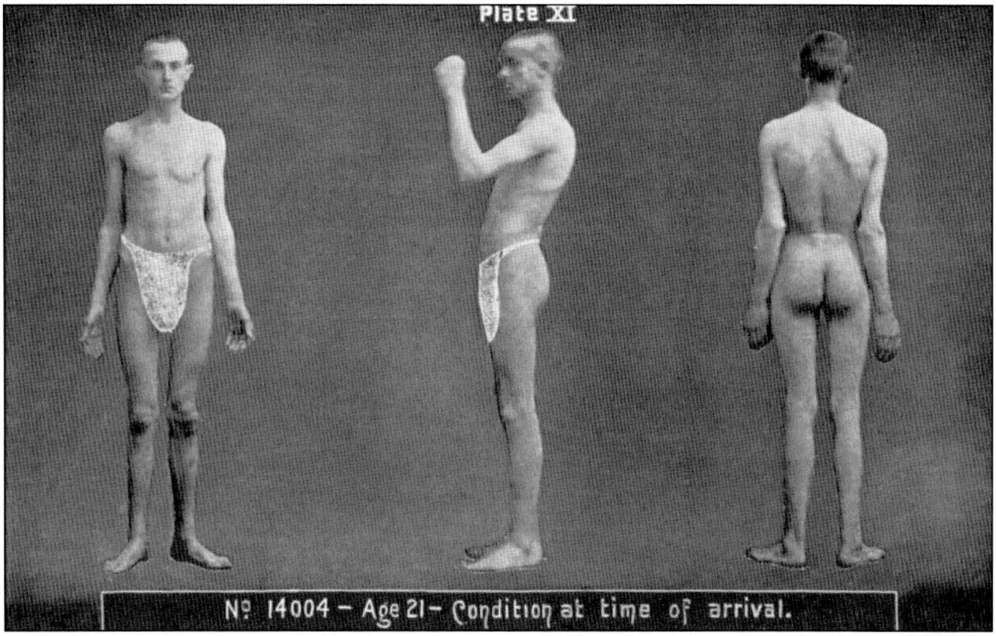


No. 14004 had a case of serious effusion in the cavity of the right chest, following epidemic influenza. After the withdrawal of the fluid (and when able to be about), he was placed in the gymnasium.

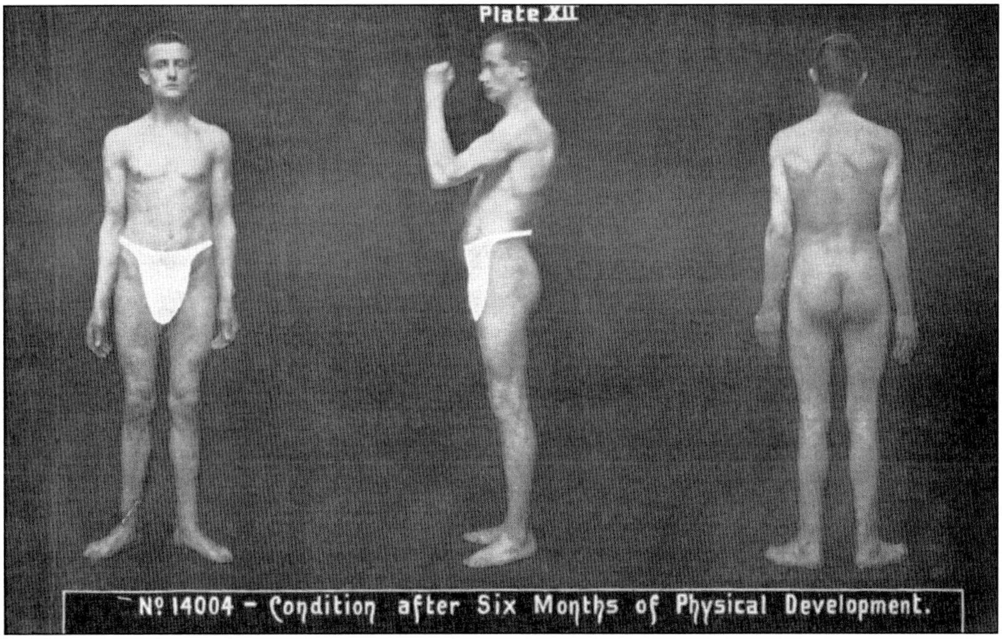


His progress there, though slow, was continuous and compared favorably with many cases of prolonged convalescence after uncomplicated influenza.

In 1893 Dr. Wey and J. R. Monks, principal of the school of letters, applied new methods to the "kindergarten class," known thereafter as the "experimental class." Apparently, the class improved both mentally and physically. Changes in the experimental class's diet were first attempted at the reformatory during 1893. In 1894, the managers of the Elmira Reformatory suggested that the qualities and quantities of food consumed were related to morality. So long as food produced certain distinct physical results and alterations in man, it had something to do with morality.

A new scientific measure was introduced at the reformatory in 1895 by Superintendent Brockway. According to him, physiology taught that for every important part of the body, of those under control of the will, there was a region of the brain by which they were controlled. These regions were known as "centers" in the brain. Based on the psycho-physical principle, Brockway announced that a special manual training for the most defective inmates was to be given under the supervision of a trained director, with the sole purpose of overcoming their defects. Work with these defectives was not at all to teach trades or to educate them in the school of letters, rather it was an attempt to cure specific mental and moral perversions. Its purpose was to restore deficiencies and to adjust and balance the functions of the mind by practice of certain selected manual processes.

# *Six*

# The Military Drill Program

The military organization was made possible, indeed necessary, by the cessation of labor in August 1888 in accordance with act 586 of the laws of 1888, the so-called Yates Law. Initially, the restrictions of the law were such that there seemed no alternative but to subject the inmates to long periods of idle confinement in their cells. However, within 48 hours after the Yates Law demanded the cessation of production (all prison labor for profit) in all penal institutions, a squad of 60 men—selected from among the inmates of the first grade, with special reference to their aptness in learning and fitness to command their fellows—was being instructed in the primary principles of military tactics. With this small body as the nucleus, an entire regimental organization (with a full quota of officers for eight companies) was built up in less than a month. The tactical course followed was the same that had been in use for nearly two decades in the US Army. According to Brockway, the prohibition of all industrial labor was found to be beneficial in every way.

In 1888, the times of drilling were so arranged that each man was ensured from five to eight hours of active exercise a day, and, as often as the weather permitted, a part of it was had in the open air. All instruction in the schools of the solider and of the company was given exclusively in the morning in the armory.

In the afternoons, battalion maneuvers of various degrees of intricacy were executed on the garrison parade ground, followed each day by a dress parade. In lieu of rifles, excellent wooden guns (made from the Springfield model) that were trimmed with iron and painted to replicate service muskets were manufactured in the trades school. They weighed six to eight pounds each, were evenly balanced, and answered their purpose quite well. The men wore mock-military uniforms according to rank. The man in this photograph is standing on the parade ground, which is what the spacious lawn within the quadrangle formed by the cell houses, domestic building, and deserted workshops had come to be known.

The local administration of the regiment was in the hands of 30 field staff and officers, with a colonel, lieutenant colonel, major, adjunct, bandmaster, one captain, and two lieutenants for each of the eight companies.

The regimental color consisted of a flag of bunting in strips of blue, black, and red, representing the colors of the uniforms of the three reformatory grades.

The records of military performance were based upon the general mark system of demeanor credits and demerits, which prevailed at the reformatory. The maximum marking attainable every month, by each inmate assigned to the regiment for satisfactory performance in that connection, was three. The same penalties attached to loss of marks in general demeanor and education applied to the military department, which had replaced industrial labor at the reformatory.

Initially, it was not expected that the military exercises would replace productive labor as a reformative means. However, it had proven so excellent a substitute as to warrant its extended trial and, perhaps, permanent adoption as a part of the reformatory system of training, even when the industrial system was resumed. The so-called Yates Law of 1888 had the practical impact of releasing all 828 inmates for direct reformatory training. Eventually placed under the command of Col. Claude F. Bryan of West Point, the reformatory became like a garrison of a thousand prisoner soldiers.

In a few months, the entire reformatory had been transformed into a military garrison governed by approximately the same regulations as were in effect at the academy at West Point. So firmly had the military regime been established, that even when the trades school was reorganized and means were found for reestablishing prison industries, it remained in place.

The military drill included setting up and marching in common and in double time. When possible, each prisoner in the regiment had from five to eight hours a day of active exercise (drill) in the open air. There was company drill in the morning and battalion drill in the afternoon.

It was the intention of the superintendent to divide all the prisoners into two battalions. Each would be drilled for two hours, once in the morning and once in the afternoon. The superintendent stated that the drill fixed the attention of the men, exercised mind and body alike, and was the best possible substitute for labor. To further employ the prisoners' time, they attended classes in calisthenics for two hours every day.

The reformatory regiment was under the command of a former prisoner who had seen service in the German army. The drill and calisthenics occupied only a part of the time and were valuable in the physical development of the prisoners. In addition, prisoners spent four hours every day in the trades schools.

According to Brockway's account, the military drill of the inmates had reached a good degree of perfection by 1889. Ten companies composed a regiment of 803 men. Every day, the unemployed inmates were drilled in the forenoon. All inmates were drilled on Wednesday and Saturday afternoons. There was a dress parade every evening at four o'clock. Every month a competitive examination was held, wherein all the companies competed for a set of badges to be worn for the month by the commissioned officers of the successful company.

Gradually, the government of the reformatory was becoming a military one, comprised largely of inmate military officers. According to Brockway, the health and bearing of the men was better, their habitual mental tone was improved, and common disciplinary difficulties diminished. The military government of the reformatory seemed almost indispensable to satisfactory management. Holding this view, Brockway appointed Claude F. Bryan, a competent military instructor, thereby making the military drills a permanent department of training and a distinguishing feature of the reformatory's disciplinary regime.

The military organization habituated the men to prompt and implicit obedience, deference to their superiors, and to the habit of command and loyalty. On Parade Avenue (pictured here), men emerged from the armory on the right and headed for the parade ground. Every able-bodied inmate was a member of the military organization. When labor was resumed, the military was found to have developed into such a valuable disciplinary adjunct that the organization was continued.

In 1890, the regimental roster contained the names of 857 men. The military instructor was the colonel of the regiment (there was also a major, an adjutant, and a sergeant major). The regiment was comprised of 10 companies, each of which had a captain, a first lieutenant, and two second lieutenants (in addition to the usual noncommissioned officers). Two afternoons in the week were set aside for military instruction, and there was a dress parade every evening on the parade ground when weather permitted. In addition, monthly competitive drill was held. Military and labor were computed as a third factor, with school and general demeanor, at the end of each month.

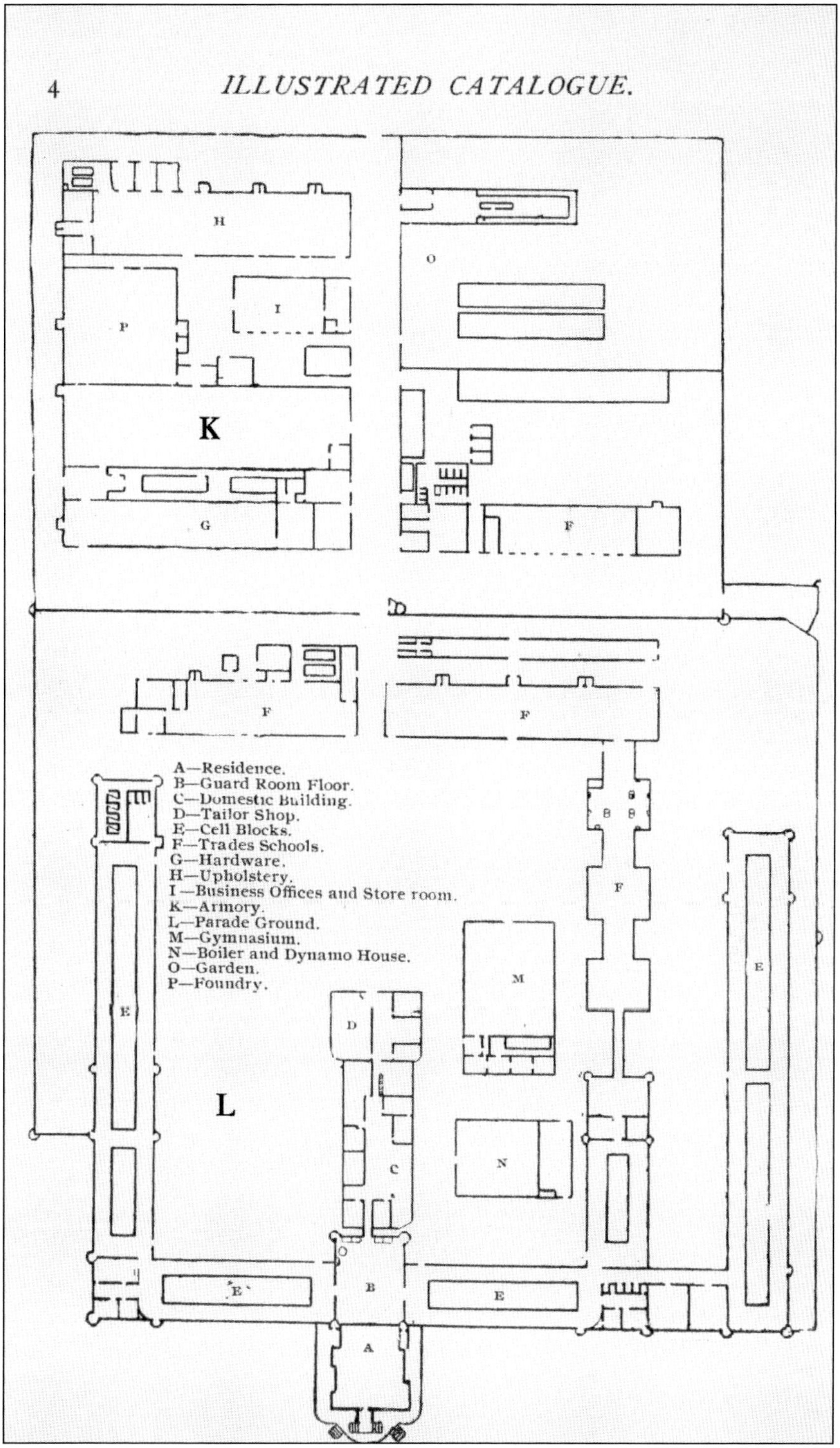


This 1890 floor plan shows the armory (K), which was provided to accommodate the equipment of the entire regiment, and the parade ground (L).

Each company had its regularly assigned place of muster at the beating of the assembly, after which all proceeded in order to the parade ground, where the battalion was assembled for dress parade or other drills. These military exhibitions attracted a great deal of attention, and as many as 200 or 300 hundred spectators often occupied the lawn during dress parade.

The reformatory's band was an invaluable adjunct to the military regiment. Occasional concerts were given to the inmates, to the apparent pleasure of others who chanced to be present. However, its primary function was to appear at dress parade, with the drum major in the lead.

The prisoners were organized as the reformatory regiment, with 10 companies and attained great proficiency. In the morning there were squad and company drills, and in the afternoon there was a dress parade. The military instructor was a West Point cadet, regularly employed by the institution, and he was the colonel of the regiment. The other officers were all prisoners in the first grade or paroled.

According to visitors and other observers, various maneuvers were executed in columns of companies. The reformatory band, composed of 24 prisoners, led the march and played some good military music. A regimental line was formed, and the command went through the silent manual of arms flawlessly.

In 1891, the drilling exercises occurred on Wednesday and Saturday afternoons from one to five o'clock. The ceremony of guard mounting was followed by company maneuvers, from setting-up movements to bayonet exercises and skirmishing, and, often, battalion drills. Regimental parade, with retreat, was held every Monday, Tuesday, Thursday, and Friday afternoon. On Wednesdays and Saturdays, the 12 companies comprising the regiment were divided into three battalions of four companies each for a brigade dress parade.

The parade ceremonies attracted as many as 500 visitors on summer afternoons. The regimental headquarters were in a building formerly used as a foundry, in which there was a clear floor space of 15,000 feet. However, this did not give sufficient area for maneuvering upwards of a thousand men.

Incentives for effort on the part of the men, beyond those furnished by the mark system, were monthly competitions between the various companies. At these competitions, which attracted large groups of outside visitors, the captains were assigned 10 movements through which to take their commands under the surveillance of critical judges.

The regimental band appeared daily at dress parade under the charge of a drum major. Occasionally, the band played a concert in the assembly hall for the entertainment of the inmate population. In addition, the wind instruments furnished the accompaniments for the choir at Sunday services.

Early in the spring of 1892, the National Guard of the state adopted a newly framed set of tactics for setting-up exercises that was approved by the US War Department.

The old system of drill was excluded from the reformatory regimental manual and the revised regulations were adopted. The chairs seen in the bottom left corner of this photograph were for visitors to sit and observe.

The only portion of the improved manual that was more lengthy and difficult than the old system was the setting-up exercises, or calisthenics, which were quadrupled.

When first organized in 1888, the reformatory regiment numbered 560 men distributed among 8 companies. During the summer of 1892, the number of recruits was multiplying in such proportions that it was resolved by management to reorganize the entire regiment. In pursuance, during the first week of July, the number of companies was increased to 16, with an average roll of 65 privates to each company.

The regiment, by this proceeding, was divided into two battalions consisting of 1,040 cadets. Two considerations entered into the formation of the various companies: individual height and grade. Upper-first or probationary grade inmates wore blue suits. Companies who were members of the lower-first or neutral-grade wore black suits, while members of the second or convict-grade wore red suits.

According to Brockway, the military system at the reformatory was the brainchild of himself and a very educated prisoner. Brockway said, "Coincidentally, almost at the moment of my own mental decision, he proposed precisely the same plan. I at once assigned him to select from the records and to nominate sixty inmates for military officers, and himself to take up the duty of training and organizing the regiment." Superintendent Brockway is shown watching a drill on June 15, 1895. In a 1900 annual report, the board of managers maintained that from a mental standpoint, the "military" possessed many merits. The system developed moral faculties by the strict conception it imparted of the value of order, government, command, obedience, and duty. In the case of the reformatory, it offered an incentive to mental and moral progress.

# *Seven*

# Prison Discipline at Elmira

The reformatory system of prison discipline developed at Elmira stands as the exemplar of the reform or medical model in penology. From the standpoint of reform at Elmira, crime was equated with ignorance and moral depravity. The course of desired behavior was specific, delimited by exacting rules, orders, and regulations, as well as by the constraints of the environment with which the offender was forced to adapt. In other words, change was external, forced, and coercive. The offender had no choice but to comply with the behavioral demands of the system if he wanted to be paroled. There was an old saying among prisoners at Elmira relative to obedience: "They will kill you on the hill." On the other hand, Elmira was also referred to as the "college on the hill." Upon admission, all prisoners at Elmira were assigned to the second or intermediate grade, with liability to fall to the third or penal grade for misconduct or promotion to the first grade by good behavior. Inmates at the reformatory were classified into three grades (the "first," "second," and "third") until 1890, when the grades changed in name to "upper-first," "first," and "second." Movement up-and-down the grading system was determined by the number of marks a prisoner earned each month. Demotion to the third grade was based on a disregard of rules or properties that showed indifference to progress or to the desire for self-control. Promotion to the first grade was accomplished by earning nine marks for each of six months in, or nearly in, succession. The marks were earned three for demeanor, three for labor, and three for progress in school. After reaching the first grade, six more months of exemplary performance was required under somewhat relaxed security conditions. When there was sufficient confidence in the inmate and outside employment had been secured, he would receive his parole. Six months of good conduct on parole would usually secure absolute release from the board of managers.

SAMPLE PAGES OF CONDUCT-BOOK.

*N. Y. S. R. Conduct Record.*

*No* 2999. *Name* John Doe. *Grade* 2

| Date | | To be Earned. | Loss. | Gain. | Balance. | REMARKS. |
|---|---|---|---|---|---|---|
| 1880. | | 387 | | | | |
| Dec. | 31 | 379 | | 8 | | 4 offences in Shop—1. |
| 1881. | | | | | | |
| Jan'y | 31 | 372 | | 7 | | 10 offences talking in Shop—2. |
| Feb'y | 28 | 366 | | 6 | | General violation of Shop rules—2. Spelling—1. |
| Mch. | 31 | 360 | | 6 | | Continual talking and fooling in Shop & line and disorderly in Chapel—1. Bad sewing—1. Spelling—1. |
| | | | | | | Reduced to 3d. Grade, April 1, '81. |
| April | 30 | 351 | | 9 | | 3 offences excused |
| | | | | | | Restored to 2d. Grade, May 1, '81 |
| May | 31 | 342 | | 9 | | |

*N. Y. S. R. Conduct Record.*

*No* 2999. *Name* John Doe. *Grade* 2

| Date. | | To be Earned | Loss. | Gain. | Balance. | REMARKS. |
|---|---|---|---|---|---|---|
| | | 342 | | | | |
| June | 30 | 333 | | 9 | | 2 offences excused |
| July | 31 | 234 | | 9 | | |
| Aug. | 31 | 316 | | 8 | | Obtaining newspaper, room disorderly—1. |
| Sept. | 30 | 307 | | 9 | | |
| Oct. | 31 | 298 | | 9 | | 1 Offence excused |
| Nov. | 30 | 289 | | 9 | | 2 Offences excused |
| Dec. | 31 | 280 | | 9 | | Promoted to 1st Grade, Dec. 1, '81 |
| 1882. | | | | | | |
| Jan'y | 31 | 271 | | 9 | | |
| Feb'y | 28 | 262 | | 9 | | 1 Offence excused |
| Mch. | 31 | 253 | | 9 | | Loss in study not to affect Grade |
| April | 30 | 244 | | 9 | | |
| May | 31 | 235 | | 9 | | Paroled, June 10, 1882. |

Every man received into the reformatory was charged with nine marks for every month of time the court, under the determinate sentencing law, had sentenced him. Thus, if he had been sentenced for five years, the possible abatement (17 months under the determinate sentencing law) would leave him 43 months to serve. Such a man was charged, under the new system, with 43 months multiplied by 9 marks, for a total of 387 marks. By maintaining perfect conduct, earning 9 marks per month, he would be released at the same time as possible under the old law. The difference under the indeterminate sentence law and the mark system was that the managers could release him at any time or grant a parole. In the example shown above, an inmate was released after serving only 17 months under the Indeterminate Sentencing Law of 1877. Under the old law, he would have served 43 months.

In 1882, under the direction of the general superintendent, the school secretary had special charge of the schools. His responsibilities included grading; supervision of the lower classes when instructed by inmate teachers; computation of percentages of the monthly examinations; and maintaining attendance records. He was also to assist in supervising the correspondence of inmates; selecting, caring for, and distributing library books and materials; and printing the conduct records kept in the guard room office.

In 1886, notice of a conduct report against an inmate was delivered to his cell as soon as possible after it was filed. If not guilty, the offender was to return the notice, accompanied by a denial and explanation, to the superintendent within 24 hours. As a general rule, reports were not investigated unless denied. Pictured is an inmate sitting in front of the disciplinary officer.

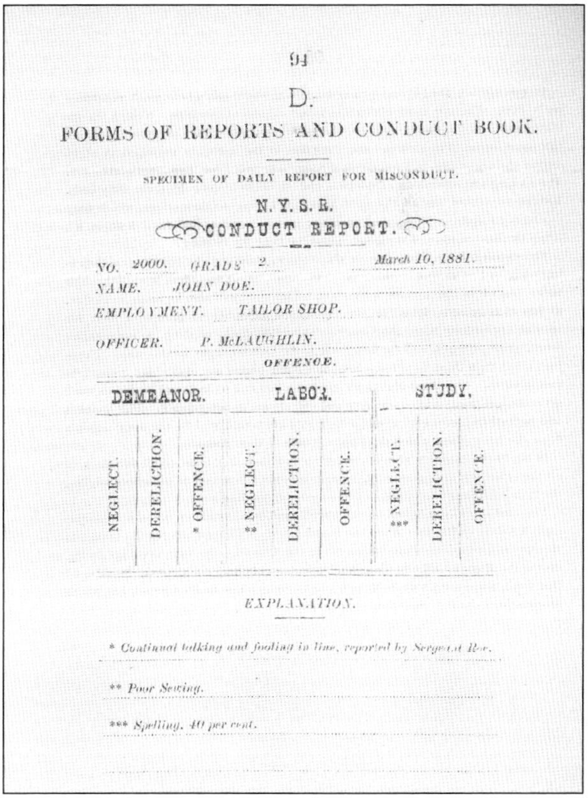

94

D.

FORMS OF REPORTS AND CONDUCT BOOK.

SPECIMEN OF DAILY REPORT FOR MISCONDUCT.

N. Y. S. R.

CONDUCT REPORT.

NO. *2000.* GRADE *2.* *March 10, 1881.*

NAME. *JOHN DOE.*

EMPLOYMENT. *TAILOR SHOP.*

OFFICER. *P. McLAUGHLIN.*

*OFFENCE.*

| DEMEANOR. | | | LABOR. | | | STUDY. | | |
|---|---|---|---|---|---|---|---|---|
| NEGLECT. | DERELICTION. | * OFFENCE. | ** NEGLECT. | DERELICTION. | OFFENCE. | *** NEGLECT. | DERELICTION. | OFFENCE. |

*EXPLANATION.*

* *Continual talking and fooling in line, reported by Sergeant Roe.*

** *Poor Sewing.*

*** *Spelling. 40 per cent.*

Marks lost because of neglect or derelict reports could eventually be restored when subsequent conduct demonstrated that the problem had been corrected.

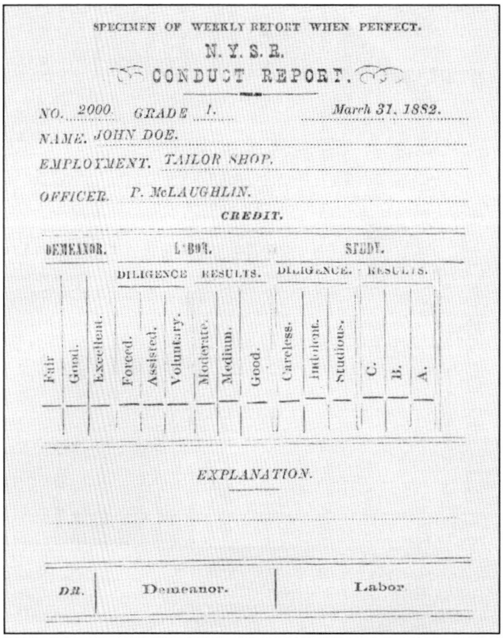
SPECIMEN OF WEEKLY REPORT WHEN PERFECT.

N. Y. S. R.

CONDUCT REPORT.

NO. 2000 GRADE 1. March 31, 1882.

NAME. JOHN DOE.

EMPLOYMENT. TAILOR SHOP.

OFFICER. P. McLAUGHLIN.

CREDIT.

| DEMEANOR. | | | LABOR. | | | | | | STUDY. | | | | | |
|---|---|---|---|---|---|---|---|---|---|---|---|---|---|---|
| | | | DILIGENCE | | | RESULTS. | | | DILIGENCE. | | | RESULTS. | | |
| Fair | Good. | Excellent. | Forced. | Assisted. | Voluntary. | Moderate. | Medium. | Good. | Careless. | Indolent. | Studious. | C. | B. | A. |
| | | | | | | | | | | | | | | |

EXPLANATION.

| DR. | Demeanor. | Labor |
|---|---|---|

Marks were earned by perfection in conduct, school, and work. At work, marks were earned by the voluntary performance of a reasonable amount of work without wastefulness and with care to produce quality products. In school, marks were earned by diligence in the studies assigned and by scoring no lower than 75 percent on all examinations. In terms of demeanor, marks were earned by obeying all the many rules and regulations of the government of the facility.

In 1891, clerks were stationed on the guardroom floor (the second story of the central building). They registered all incidents relating to the conduct, labor, and study of each inmate; recorded his earnings with the charges against him for board, clothes, and fines; and kept exhaustive memoranda (easily referred to and understood) of every incident that affected him—every privilege granted and every penalty imposed.

In 1886, the transfer officer was to transport all newly convicted offenders from the county jail to the reformatory. He was further charged with maintaining the records of paroled prisoners, supervising all prisoners paroled within the state, and corresponding with all paroled prisoners (to the end that he may be informed of their activities).

New inmates were immediately cleansed, clothed in a second-grade suit, photographed, described in the admissions register, and given a medical examination. Next, he was thoroughly questioned by the general superintendent for the "biographical record" to ascertain the causes of his crime and the particular culture required for his cure.

As of 1882, custody officers lived on the grounds of the reformatory. They were not permitted to leave the premises without permission or be absent at night after 11 o'clock.

Prison officers were to be constantly observant of the mental condition of the prisoners, noting any changes in their mood, conduct, or appearance that might indicate the onset of depression or unusual irritability.

The principal keeper had, under the direction of the general superintendent, the responsibility of the safe custody and proper discipline of the inmates, as well as the control and direction of the officers under his direct supervision. Furthermore, he was required to keep a daily journal and had general charge of the details of the financial administration of the security operation. Pictured is the principal keeper's office in the guardroom.

The officers' common area in the guardroom was a place for custody officers to relax.

The hall keeper had oversight of the cells, rooms, corridors, hospital, and patients; clothing and bedding; the admission and discharge of all prisoners; communication between inmates and all persons outside of the reformatory, including family and friends; and of the keys, weapons, and institutional stores in general.

The evident intention of the Fassett Law, passed in 1889, was that chronic criminals should be employed in some fashion. Believing that there were but few of this class at the reformatory, the superintendent, with the approval of the board of managers, rechristened the grades. Instead of first, second, and third grade prisoners, they were classed as first, lower first, and second, thus allowing the employment of all upon educational industries. In 1892, the board of managers held meetings quarterly—in the last weeks of January, April, July, and October—to consider the cases of those who were eligible for parole.

Release was not granted until the inmate secured employment on the outside. If the terms of the conditional release were complied with for a period of six months, the board of managers granted absolute release. Pictured is Supt. Zebulon Brockway, who was responsible to the board of managers, was a member of the parole board, and attended all board meetings.

FORM OF PAROLE.

The Act of 1877, Chapter 173, Section 8, is as follows, viz:

"The said Board of Managers shall have power to establish rules and regulations under which prisoners within the Reformatory may be allowed to go upon parole outside of the Reformatory buildings and enclosure, but to remain, while on parole in the legal custody and under control of the Board of Managers, and subject at any time to be taken back within the enclosure of said Reformatory, and full power to enforce such rules and regulations and to retake and reimprison any convict so upon parole, is hereby conferred upon said Board, whose order certified by its secretary, shall be a sufficient warrant for all officers named in it to authorize such officer to return to actual custody any conditionally released or paroled prisoner, and it is hereby made the duty of all officers to execute said order the same as ordinary criminal process. * * * * *"

NEW YORK STATE REFORMATORY

AT ELMIRA, N. Y.

PAROLE.

| | | | |
|---|---|---|---|
| *Name* | *John Doe.* | *Crime* | *Burglary 3d. Degree.* |
| *Age.* | 20. | *Date of Sentence* | *Nov.* 30, 1880. |
| *Height* | 5:9. | *Date when Admitted* | *Dec.* 6, 1880. |
| *Weight* | 155 *lbs.* | *Date of Parole* | *June* 10, 1882. |
| *Complexion* | *Fair.* | *County* | *N. Y. City.* |
| *Eyes* | *Blue.* | *Court* | *Gen'l Sessions.* |
| *Hair* | *Brown.* | *Occupation* | *Carpenter.* |
| *Marks* | *None.* | *Residence* | 180 *W.* 20*th St.* |

The Managers having confidence in your purpose to become a good citizen, and desiring to test your strength of character and ability to fulfill your purpose, do now, by virtue of the authority conferred upon them by Law, grant and order this Parole, under the following Rules and Regulations:

1. You shall proceed directly to the place of Employment provided for you viz: Blank Foundry Co., Narrowsburg, N. Y.. and there remain, if practicable, for at least six months from this date.

2. You shall on the first of every month, for a period of six months or more, and until absolutely released by the Managers, forward by mail to the General Superintendent, a report of yourself, certified to by your employer, or Henry Black Esq., the Agent of the Managers, which report shall state whether you have been constantly under pay during the month, and if not, why not, and how much money you have earned, and how much you have expended or saved, together with a general and full statement of yourself and surroundings.

3. In case you find it desirable to change your employment or residence, you shall first get consent of the Managers through the General Superintendent.

This was the original parole document from 1879, provided by chapter 173, section 8 of the laws of 1877.

4. You shall in all respects, conduct yourself with honesty, sobriety and decency; avoiding low or evil associations; and you shall abstain from intoxicating drinks.

5. ........................................................................................

..........................................................................................

..........................................................................................

..........................................................................................,

..........................................................................................

The Government of the Reformatory has a lively and friendly interest in you both for your own sake and for the sake of society. You need not fear to communicate with the General Superintendent in case you lose your situation or become unable to labor by reason of sickness.

During the period of this Parole, you may rely upon the aid and counsel of the Managers and Superintendent, and may find the Reformatory a desirable retreat in case of disaster.

} Managers.

By the Managers:

*General Superintendent.*

Dated.

This was the original parole document from 1879, continued from the image on the left.

NEW YORK STATE REFORMATORY.

## PAROLED MAN'S ABSOLUTE RELEASE.

To ..........................................................................................

At the .............................................................................. meeting of the Managers, your Absolute Release was authorized to take effect ..............................

..............................................

Having earned your parole by good performance while here, and having since shown you ability to maintain yourself and your character in ordinary society, there is no reason to prevent your becoming a well-to-do, respected and useful citizen. Your Absolute Release is ordered in the expectation that such will be your success.

By the Managers:

This was the form signed by the board of managers and the superintendent releasing a man from parole.

F.

## RULES RELATING TO SPECIAL CLASSES OF INMATES.

1. Paroled men, who through *misfortune* or *inability*, lose place and voluntarily return with our advice and consent, but without arrest or formal order, to be received as guests and again placed as soon as may be—with exceptions.

2. Paroled men, who through *fault, but without crime*, lose place and voluntarily come in on our request or order, to be placed in second grade for three months at least, and then to go through the first grade in the ordinary way—with exceptions.

3. Paroled men, who violate their paroles by gross improprieties or by crime, who are apparently in the way to commit crimes, when arrested and brought in, to be placed in the second or third grade, as the case may be adjudged on admission, and to work through to release in the ordinary way—with exceptions.

4. Other inmates who escape or attempt to escape, to be degraded to the third grade and remain in such grade as they shall prove worthy of, until the "good time" expiration of their maximum term *at least*.

5. Ex-convicts (not necessarily including misdemeanants).

(A) Those who acknowledge the fact of their previous imprisonment immediately on admission, or who voluntarily make it known afterwards, to be detained until the "good time" expiration of their maximum term—with exceptions when the maximum is very great.

(B) Those who under peculiar pressure reveal the fact of their former imprisonment, or when it is ascertained without their acknowledgement, to be detained until the full expiration of their maximum term—with exceptions when the maximum is too great.

[Note.] Any inmate may be transferred to the State Prison, for cause on Managers' order and Superintendent of Prison's consent, and will there serve out the full maximum of his possible imprisonment here. If transferred, he can earn no good time in the State Prison.

These rules applied to special classes of inmates as first provided for in 1879.

In 1884, the Ohio Legislature enacted a general indeterminate sentence and parole law regulating its penitentiary.

Indiana established a reformatory in 1897. By 1892, seven states had established reformatories based on the model provided by the Elmira Reformatory. That number increased over the next few decades until almost every state in the country had a reformatory.

The 1894 New York State Constitution provided for a state commission of prisons consisting of eight gubernatorial appointees. By chapter 1026 of the laws of 1895, the legislature transferred oversight of the Elmira Reformatory from the New York State Board of Charities to the New York State Commission of Prisons. On July 31, 1900, Z.R. Brockway resigned as general superintendent at the request of the managers. In 1901, the membership of the state commission of prisons was reduced to three appointees, and the commissioners were assigned to serve also as the board of commissioners for paroled prisoners. In 1906, the legislature created a state board of managers of reformatories to manage both Elmira and the Eastern New York Reformatory at Napanoch. According to chapter 684, section 1 of the laws of 1906, the state reformatory at Elmira was to be known as the New York State Reformatory.

The board of commissioners for paroled prisoners, abolished in 1908, was replaced by a board of parole for state prisons independent of the state commission of prisons. The membership of the state commission of prisons was increased to seven gubernatorial appointees. By chapter 606, section 400 of the laws of 1926, the legislature created a department of correction and placed the management of Elmira under the commissioner of correction. The name of the New York State Commission of Prisons was changed to the New York State Commission of Correction. The commissioner of the new commission of correction became the chairperson as well. Placed administratively within the department of correction, the commission of correction nevertheless retained independent powers of visitation and inspection. According to chapter 606, section 412 of the laws of 1926, the board of managers was to be known as the board of visitors. Under chapter 151 of the laws of 1933, the name New York State Reformatory, located at Elmira, was changed back to Elmira Reformatory. There continued to be a board of visitors consisting of seven members appointed by the governor.

By chapter 475, section 5 of the laws of 1970, the reformatory name was changed again to the Elmira Correctional Facility when the new department of correctional services was established in 1970. The designation "reformatory" was legislated out of existence, and the rationale for punishment was changed from reform to rehabilitation. In 1973, the commission of correction was established as an independent agency within the executive department (under article 3 of the New York State correction law). The commission functioned with part-time members until 1975 (chapter 865), when the present commission with three full-time members and other staff was established.

In his book *The History of the Elmira Reformatory*, published in 1891, Alexander Winter referred to Elmira as a "moral hospital of over 1,000 inmates, unlike any other prison in the world." From 1876 to 1900, Elmira was the embodiment of the medical model under the leadership of Zebulon Brockway. His departure in 1900 came in the wake of persistent accusations of cruelty in his treatment of prisoners. In addition, it was alleged that Brockway exaggerated the success of turning around the lives of young offenders. Within a few decades of Brockway's departure, the reformatory movement had run its course and was replaced by rehabilitation as the dominant rationale for the punishment of criminals in the United States. Training in the machine shop and other trades school classes continued at Elmira during the rehabilitation era of prison discipline. Prisoners were trained in metal-turning operations, milling operations, drilling operations, and metal burnishing.

The rehabilitation rationale for punishment that developed in the 1930s in America was largely in response to the alleged failure of the reformatory system of prison discipline to either reform criminals or to reduce crime.

From the standpoint of the rehabilitation rationale, the object of punishment was to intervene in the life of the offender rather than to cure him or her of some physical, mental, or moral defect.

According to the rehabilitation rationale (often referred to as the "treatment model'), crime was equated with social problems, such as poverty and unemployment.

In correctional institutions, the emphasis was to be on helping the offender identify his problems and develop more mature social relations.

Under the reformatory system of prison discipline, the offender had no choice but to submit to the treatment programs chosen for him by reformatory staff. In contrast, under the rehabilitation system of prison discipline, prisoners were involved with staff in the treatment development process and were allowed, for the most part, to choose what type of treatment program in which they wanted to participate.

In this photograph, a brick masonry student works with his instructor.

Artist Ernfred Anderson mounted separately casted fig leaves onto this statue at Elmira to make it less objectionable. It was placed at its current location in 1951.

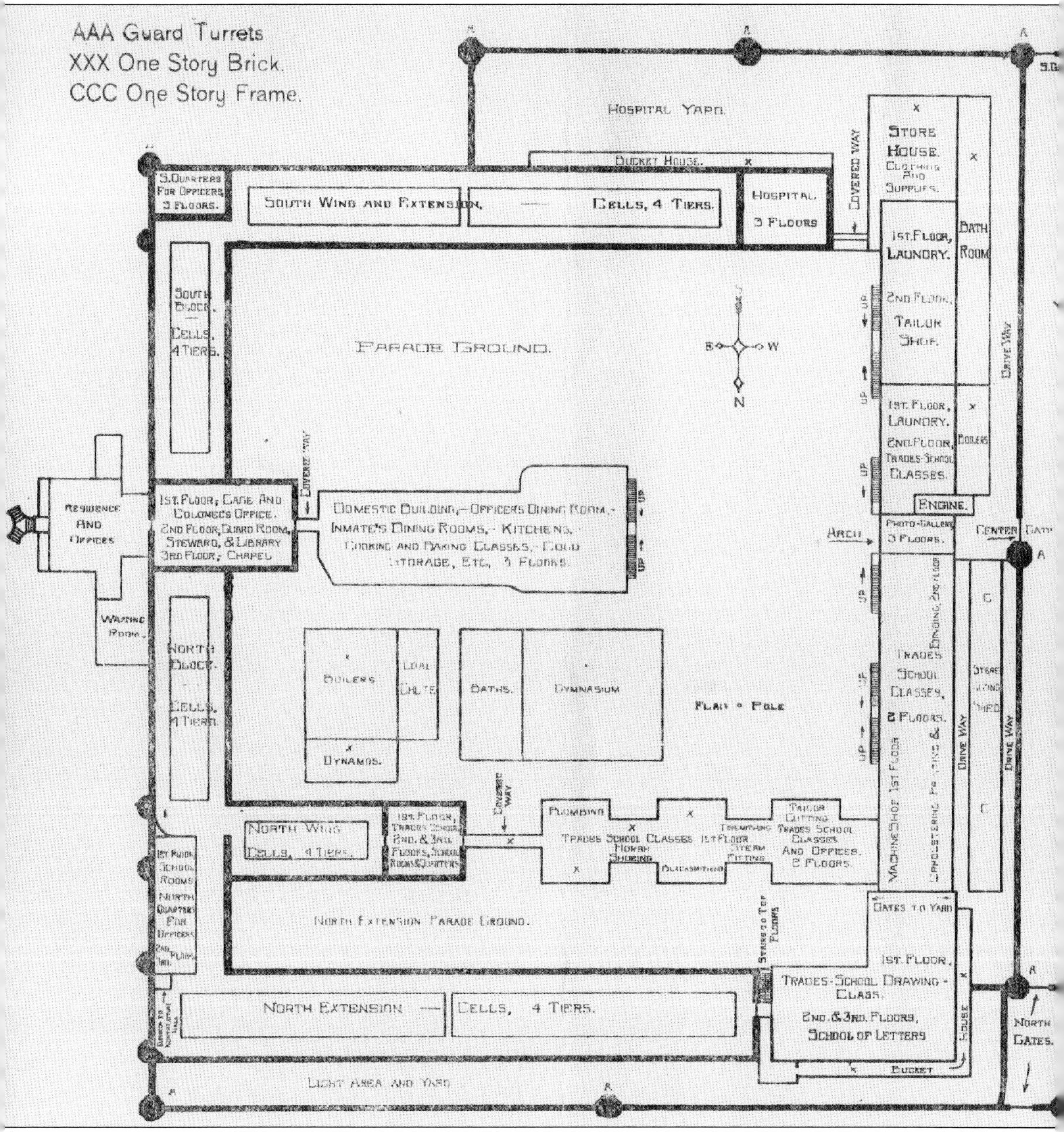


This 1901 ground plan of the eastern half of the institution shows the addition of new buildings and facilities (compared to the 1891 ground plan).

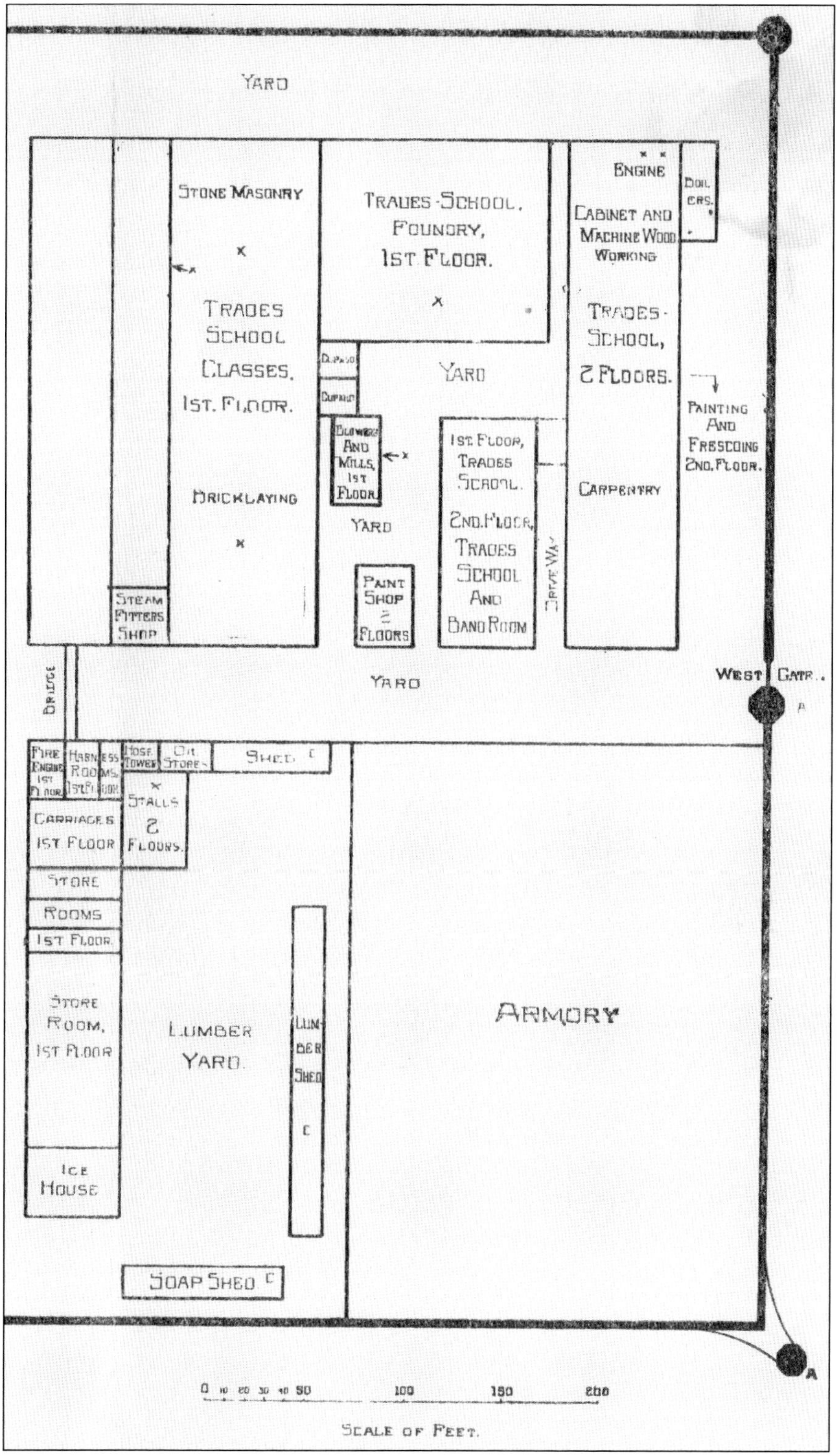


Pictured is the western half of the ground plan of the institution in 1901.

Consistent with our mission to preserve history on a local level, this book was printed in South Carolina on American-made paper and manufactured entirely in the United States. Products carrying the accredited Forest Stewardship Council (FSC) label are printed on 100 percent FSC-certified paper.

MADE IN THE USA